THE BIBLE LAND

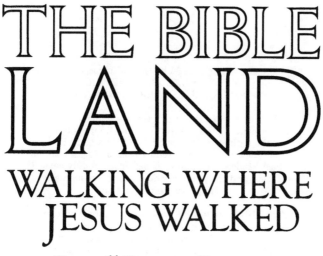

THE BIBLE LAND

WALKING WHERE JESUS WALKED

Batsell Barrett Baxter

Harold Hazelip

Bill Humble

CHRISTIAN COMMUNICATIONS
P.O.BOX 150
NASHVILLE, TN 37202

Photographs are by Bill Humble. Used by permission.

Published by Christian Communications
A division of the Gospel Advocate Co.
P.O. Box 150, Nashville, TN 37202

ISBN 0-89225-323-1

Second Printing, June 1990

CONTENTS

CHAPTER ONE

The Land in Old Testament Days

St. Catherine's Monastery at the base of Mt. Sinai was built by Emperor Justinian in 6th century.   1.1

Mount Sinai

Harold Hazelip

Background Reading: *Exodus 19:1–21; Exodus 32:1–35*

One may reach Mount Sinai by private plane or he may drive. Political control of the Sinai Peninsula reverts from Israel to Egypt as a result of the 1979 peace agreements.

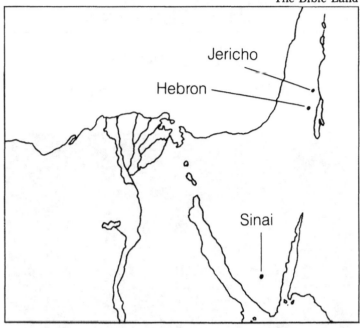

The Sinai Peninsula is a triangle of land with the "base" of the triangle at the top. It stretches some 150 miles from the Gulf of Suez on the west to the Gulf of Aqaba on the east. The triangle also stretches about 260 miles from the Mediterranean Sea on the north to the northern end of the main body of the Red Sea on the south.

The terrain of the area ranges from shifting sand dunes to bare rock and hard-baked soil to naked, craggy mountains. A few palm groves and oases dot the area. The night air is cool but the day may bring temperatures to 120° Fahrenheit.

The books of Exodus and Numbers mention five wilderness areas: the wilderness of Shur in the northwest, east of Goshen; the wilderness of Etham between the Bitter Lakes and Marah; the wilderness of Sin near Elim in the western Sinai; the wilderness of Paran near the Gulf of Aqaba; and the wilderness of Zin near

Kadesh-barnea, along what would later be the border of Judah.

The Sinai Peninsula has been a highway for travelers that include Abraham and Sarah; young Joseph, who had been sold by his brothers; and Mary, Joseph, and Jesus during Jesus' early childhood. Moses and the Israelites wandered for forty years in the area. Camel caravans laden with rich goods going from one part of the Fertile Crescent to another knew the area. The Sinai has a population of 35,000 today.

The word *Sinai* appears thirty-seven times in Scripture, *Horeb* seventeen times. No geographical distinction between these terms is noted in the Bible. Elijah went to Horeb in his flight from Ahab and Jezebel (1 Kings 19:4–8). It was an eleven-day journey from Kadesh-barnea at the southern edge of Palestine to Horeb (Deut. 1:2).

Israel's Route

The exodus did not take Israel along any of the well-traveled roads. This makes it difficult for modern geographers to trace their route with certainty. The Israelites began at Rameses (Num. 33:5), the capital city which Raamses II built. They left Egypt "by the way of the wilderness toward the Red Sea" (Exod. 13:18), but the exact place of the crossing is not known. Instead of taking one of the direct roads eastward, the Israelites traveled through the desert, making stops at Marah where bitter waters were made sweet (Exod. 15:23–26) and at the oasis of Elim (Exod. 15:27) with its twelve springs and seventy palm trees.

They also stopped at Dophkah, which has been identified with the copper and turquoise mining area operated by the pharaohs. Their last stop before Mount Sinai was at Rephidim, where Moses struck the rock, bringing forth water (Exod. 17:1–7), and Israel fought

9

the Amalekites under Joshua's leadership (Exod. 17:8–16).

Israel at Sinai

The Israelites reached Mount Sinai in the third month after their departure from Egypt and camped at its foot where they could view the summit (Exod. 19:1, 16–20). God revealed himself to Moses, who then called on the people to make a covenant with God (Exod. 19:1–8). When Israel agreed to keep God's words, they were given three days to prepare themselves before the beginning of the events which brought the Ten Commandments and the accompanying laws. The people later heard the law read (Exod. 24:3, 7) and watched as Moses built an altar and sacrificed to the Lord (24:4–6). A group composed of Moses, Aaron, Nadab, Abihu, and seventy of the elders of Israel are described as going up and seeing the God of Israel standing on a pavement of sapphire (Exod. 24:9–11). Moses took Joshua into the mountain and stayed forty days; here he was shown the pattern of the tabernacle (Exod. 24:12—31:18).

When Moses returned from the mountain, the people had grown weary with his long absence and had fashioned a golden calf (Exod. 32:1–6). Moses had to persuade God not to slay them (Exod. 32:7–14). Moses destroyed the golden calf and broke the tablets of the law (Exod. 32:15–24). Moses stood at the gate of the camp and asked, "Who is on the Lord's side? Come to me." The Levites responded and were ordered to put to death the idolaters (Exod. 32:25–29). The camp of Israel was hit with a plague (Exod. 32:30–35).

After telling Israel to prepare to leave Sinai and go to the Promised Land and after instructing Moses to set up the tent of meeting, God gave Moses a second set of the stone tablets and revealed several other commands and warnings (Exod. 33–34). After other instructions (Leviticus), the people prepared for the march (Num. 1–10). A census was taken, leaders were appointed in each tribe, the Levites were organized, camp regulations were spelled out, including details about the order of marching; and the people left Sinai (Num. 10:11–13).

In the area around the traditional site of the giving of the law, three mountains tower over the plain: Mount Catherine rises 8,536 feet above sea level on the southwest; Mount Moses 7,363 feet; and Ras es-Safsaf 6,540 feet on the northwest. Several traditional sites have been chosen through the centuries, but none is certain. At 6,900 feet on Jebel Musa (Mount Moses) is the Chapel of Elijah (1 Kings 19:8ff.). Also on the side of this mount is the spring which is said to be the place where Moses tended Jethro's flock (Exod. 2:15ff.).

On the northwest slope of Mount Moses, Constantine's mother, Helena, built a small church in the fourth century. The Monastery of St. Catherine, covering about the size of a city block and resembling a fortress, was built on the site of Helena's church and can be traced back to the emperor Justinian in A.D. 527. The monastery library is said by some to be the oldest library in the world. It includes an invaluable list of ancient manuscripts in Greek, Syriac, Georgian, Slavic, and Arabic. The Codex Sinaiticus, a third-century Greek translation of the Bible, was found here and transferred by Konstantin von Tischendorf to the private libraries of the czars in the middle of the nineteenth century. It was later sold to the British Museum.

The monastery was founded to mark the spot where Moses saw the burning bush (Exod. 3). It encloses the Church of St. Catherine, the Chapel of the Burning Bush, and many recent buildings, including a mosque. A government-operated museum is housed a couple of miles to the west of the monastery.

After the encampment at Sinai, Moses and the Israelites moved northeastward and traveled through the wilderness of Paran. It was to this area that Hagar and Ishmael had fled (Gen. 21:21) and from the same region that the spies were sent out (Num. 10:12; 12–16). On the northern border of the wilderness of Paran is the city of Kadesh-barnea. The Israelites' exact itinerary is traced in Numbers 10–12 and 33:16f. Among the stops mentioned are Taberah, where those who murmured against the Lord were consumed by fire (Num. 11:1–3, location unknown), and Kibroth-hattaavah, where those who overate the quail died. At Hazeroth, Miriam and Aaron criticized Moses for his marriage to an Ethiopian woman.

The Sinai is still a bleak, forbidding area, but travel there today is easier than ever before.

Tomb of the Patriarchs at Hebron. 1.2

Hebron

Batsell Barrett Baxter

Background Reading: *Genesis 23:1–20; 2 Samuel 2:1–7; 2 Samuel 15:7–12*

The city of Hebron is located nineteen miles southwest of Jerusalem and about thirteen miles southwest of Bethlehem. It is 3,040 feet above sea level, which makes it the highest city in Israel. Hebron is identified with the Arab city of el-Khalil, which means "the friend of God." This may have some connection with the references in Isaiah 41:8 and James 2:23. Hebron was also known as Kiriath-arba, which means "city of four." According to Jewish tradition, it was so named because four patriarchs—Adam, Abraham, Isaac, and Jacob—were buried there. It is also known as Mamre, after the name of one of the three men who joined with Abram when he went to rescue Lot from Chedorlaomer (Gen. 14:13ff.). The other men who assisted Abram were Aner and Eshcol. According to Numbers 13, the twelve spies brought back a huge cluster of grapes from the Valley of Eshcol. A large number of springs and wells in the area make it possible for apple, plum, fig, pomegranate, apricot, and nut trees to grow. Vegetables, grapes, and melons are also produced in the area's rich soil.

Hebron is mentioned only in the Old Testament, where it occurs some sixty-one times. Kiriath-arba is mentioned six times in the Old Testament, while the oaks or plain of Mamre is mentioned another ten times. Abram moved from the Negeb to Bethel, where strife arose between his herdsmen and those of Lot. Lot moved to Sodom, and Abram moved to Hebron. It was here that his name was changed to Abraham (Gen. 17:5). While sitting at the door of his tent at the oaks of Mamre, Abraham entertained heavenly visitors whose

13

promise of a son caused Sarah to laugh (Gen. 18:1–15). They also warned Abraham of the coming destruction of Sodom and Gomorrah (Gen. 18:16–21). After the angels left, Abraham interceded to God for Sodom (Gen. 18:22–33). Afterward Abraham returned to the territory of the Negeb (Gen. 20:1).

Early History

While Abraham was grazing his flocks at Beersheba, Sarah died in Hebron and Abraham came to mourn her passing (Gen. 23:1, 2). Needing to secure an appropriate burial place for Sarah, he entered into negotiations with Ephron the Hittite to purchase the field in which was located the cave of Mach-pelah. He bought it for four hundred shekels of silver, and there buried Sarah. Later, he was also buried in the cave (Gen. 25:7–11). In the course of time Isaac and Rebekah, Jacob and Leah, and others were buried there.

Entrance to the cave of Mach-pelah has been a point of contention for centuries. A decree by the Mamelukes in 1266 forbade Jews from entering the cave. The closest the Jews could get was the seventh step of the staircase leading up to the mosque known as the Haram el-Khalil, which means "sacred precinct of the friend of the merciful one, God." The law was rescinded in 1967. Since that time the mosque has been opened to Jews and the general public. Inside the Mohammedan mosque today, surprisingly, there is a Jewish synagogue; and within close proximity of each other Muslims, Jews, and Christians come to pay their tribute to the patriarchs and their wives. The name *Mach-pelah* occurs six times in the Scriptures.

Sometime in his old age, Isaac moved to Hebron and was buried there (Gen. 35:27–29). The Bible does not specify the exact time when Jacob moved to Hebron. Apparently, Joseph had his dreams of superiority there, encountering his brothers' hatred. It was from

Hebron that he was sent to visit with his brothers in Shechem (Gen. 37:1–14). It was to Hebron that they brought their evil report concerning Joseph's death and presented to their father Jacob the blood-stained coat of Joseph (Gen. 37:15–35). Later, when Jacob and his family were in Egypt he charged his sons shortly before his death to bury him with his fathers in the cave of Mach-pelah; and this they ultimately did (Gen. 50:12–14).

Under Joshua the Israelites began to conquer the land. When Hebron had been conquered, Caleb approached Joshua at Gilgal and rehearsed to him the role he had played when, as a forty-year-old man, he was one of the twelve spies whom Moses had sent into the land. Now, at age eighty-five, Caleb reminded Joshua of Moses' promise to him and asked that he be given Hebron. Joshua granted his wish (Josh. 14:13). Hebron was also one of the six cities of refuge (Josh. 20:7) as well as a city of the Levites (Josh. 21:11–13).

David's First Capital

Hebron also played an important role in the life of King David. After the death of Saul, David asked the Lord to which of the cities of Judah he should go. God instructed him to go to Hebron; the men of Judah anointed him king there (2 Sam. 2:1–4). Hebron was the capital of David's kingdom for seven-and-one-half years, during which time six of his sons were born, including Absalom and Adonijah (2 Sam. 3:2–5). During this time Ishbosheth ruled the other tribes. The captain of his army, Abner, defected and came to David, but he was treacherously killed by Joab at the gate of the city. David put on clothes of mourning and walked behind the coffin as it moved through the streets of Hebron to the cemetery. When Ish-bosheth was assassinated by two of his own captains, David had them killed because of their treachery. After Ish-bosheth's death, David moved his capital from Hebron to Jerusalem (2 Sam. 5:1–13). Later, Hebron became the headquarters for Absalom's revolt against his father, David (2 Sam. 15:7–10).

Archaeological discovery indicates that Hebron was occupied as early as 3300 B.C. In the Amarna Letters "a field of Abram" is listed among the cities conquered by one of the pharaohs. According to Josephus, Judas Maccabaeus captured, burned, and destroyed the city. Crusaders occupied the area, but in A.D. 1187 it was returned to the Muslims, under whose control it has remained until recent years. Few cities have had so influential a role in biblical history as Hebron.

Modern tourists are reminded constantly of the story of the cluster of grapes brought back from Hebron (or the Valley of Eshcol) because a cluster of grapes is the

Herod the Great's winter palace at Jericho was recently discovered by archaeologists.   1.3

official emblem of the Israeli Department of Tourism, appearing on hundreds of vehicles, on numerous signs, and in much printed material. While visitors are not allowed to go into the depths of the cave of Mach-pelah, it is a moving experience to stand only a few feet above the place where Abraham, Isaac, Jacob, and their wives were buried.

Jericho
Harold Hazelip

Background Reading: *Joshua 2:1–14; Joshua 6:26; 1 Kings 16:34*

Jericho was the major city of the southern end of the Jordan Valley. Located at the western end of the plain, Old Testament Jericho is identified with Tell es-Sultan on the northwest outskirts of modern Jericho. The mound contains about ten acres and is four hundred yards long from north to south. New Testament Jericho is located one mile west of the modern city.

Jericho is some ten miles from the point where the Jordan empties into the Dead Sea and about seventeen miles northeast of Jerusalem. A copious spring is located at the foot of the mound. Jericho is 820 feet below sea level.

Jericho is mentioned sixty-three times in the Bible, often with reference to the plains of Jericho. When Moses was taken up into the mountain to die, and was shown the land, the city of Jericho is specifically mentioned (Deut. 34:3). Jericho was on the border of Benjamin and Ephraim. Gilgal was located on the east border of Jericho (Josh. 4:19).

Israel Conquers Jericho

Joshua sent two spies to Jericho from his headquarters at Shittim. They lodged at the home of Rahab the

17

harlot. Word reached the king of Jericho, who ordered the woman to hand over the men. She had hidden the men but told the king they had left at dark. She claimed not to know where they went but suggested that quick action might overtake them. Actually the two spies were hidden on Rahab's roof under the flax which was stored there.

The king sent men to search for the spies as far as the Jordan ford. Meanwhile, Rahab was bargaining with the spies. She had heard of the Red Sea crossing and the defeat of kings Sihon and Og. She asked to be remembered when the attack on Jericho came. The spies accepted her proposal, saying, "Our life for yours!" and promised that she and her relatives would be safe (Josh. 2:1–14).

Rahab let the spies down by a rope through her window. She advised them to go west for three days until the king's police came back. The men gave her a scarlet cord to tie to her window. This would afford her protection when the Israelites came against the city. As the men left, Rahab tied the cord in the window. The spies reported to Joshua, "Truly the Lord has given all the land into our hands; and moreover all the inhabitants of the land are fainthearted because of us" (Josh. 2:15–24).

As Joshua later stood by Jericho, the commander of the army of the Lord appeared to him. Joshua was told to take off his shoes because he stood on holy ground. He removed his shoes, bowed down, and worshiped (Josh. 5:13–15).

The city of Jericho was shut up as Israel approached. God commanded Israel to march around the city once each day for six days. Seven priests with seven trumpets of rams' horns were to go before the ark. In front of the seven priests were armed men, and the rear guard came after the ark, while the trumpets blew continually. For six days the people marched, retiring to their camp each night. Finally, on the seventh day, they went around the city seven times beginning at dawn. And they shouted and the walls of Jericho fell. The gold, silver, iron, and bronze were to go into the Lord's treasury. The people were to keep no spoil for themselves, but were to destroy the city, its men and women, and its animals. And the city was destroyed, except for the family of Rahab. The two spies who had met Rahab were charged with her rescue. She and her family were saved and went to live with Israel (Josh. 6:1–25).

After the destruction of Jericho, Joshua said, "Cursed before the Lord be the man that rises up and rebuilds this city, Jericho. At the cost of his first-born shall he lay its foundation, and at the cost of his youngest son shall he set up its gates" (Josh. 6:26). Years later during the reign of Ahab (874–853 B.C.) Hiel of Bethel rebuilt Jericho. Joshua's curse was fulfilled (1 Kings 16:34).

As Joshua took other cities and kingdoms, it was often said that he did to the king of a certain city as he did to the king of Jericho (Josh. 8:2; 10:1, 28, 30).

From Jericho Joshua sent spies to Ai. They returned and told Joshua that two or three thousand men would be sufficient to take the city. Joshua issued the order, the army set out and attacked, but was repelled (Josh. 7:1–5). Joshua was driven to prayer and learned that the reason for the defeat was the presence of sin in the camp. It was finally learned that Achan had taken as spoil from Jericho a beautiful mantle from Shinar, two hundred shekels of silver, and a gold bar weighing fifty shekels (Josh. 7:6–26).

It is not clear when the people left Jericho. After their unsuccessful attack on Ai, the entire army went to the area and seized and destroyed the city. They built an altar at Mount Ebal (Josh. 8:30–35). Later, Joshua's headquarters were at Gilgal (Josh. 14:6) and then at Shiloh (Josh. 18:1). Whether some of the people camped at Jericho during the conquest of the land is not stated.

During the lifetimes of Elijah and Elisha, a school of prophets lived at the Jericho that Hiel built. While Elisha tarried at Jericho, the men of the city asked his aid because the water of the city was bad, making the land unproductive. Elisha asked for a new bowl with salt in it. He threw salt into the spring and said, "Thus says the Lord, I have made this water wholesome; henceforth neither death nor miscarriage shall come from it" (2 Kings 2:4, 5, 15, 19–22). "Elisha's Spring" is pointed out to the modern visitor to Jericho.

Jericho in the New Testament

Herod the Great expanded the new Jericho, established some years before by Greek settlers, into a winter capital. Its climate is normally warm and pleasant, offering an improvement over the chilly, damp winters of Jerusalem.

Near Jericho a blind beggar by the name of Bartimaeus was sitting by the roadside when Jesus passed. The beggar heard a crowd passing and asked what was happening. He began to cry, "Jesus, Son of David, have mercy on me." Jesus heard him and told the people to call him. The blind man threw off his mantle, sprang up, and came to Jesus. Jesus said, "What do you want me to do for you?" Bartimaeus replied, "Master, let me receive my sight." Jesus told him to go his way for his faith had healed him. He received his sight and followed Jesus (Mark 10:46–52).

In response to a lawyer's question about the identity of one's neighbor, Jesus told a story of a man making a trip from Jerusalem to Jericho. The man was beaten, robbed, and stripped. His predicament was first witnessed by a priest and then a Levite. Both continued on their way without stopping. A Samaritan was the next to happen by. He had compassion on the man, dressed his wounds, administered medicine, and set him on his own beast. He paid the man's expenses at an inn and promised to check back. The neighbor in the story was the one who showed mercy (Luke 10:25–37).

Wealthy Zacchaeus was the head tax-collector in Jericho. When Jesus came to town the rather short Zacchaeus wanted to see the famous teacher. He went ahead of Jesus and chose a sycamore tree from which he could get a better view. Soon Jesus came to the tree where Zacchaeus was perched and spoke to him: "Zacchaeus, make haste and come down; for I must stay at your house today." Zacchaeus responded joyfully. The townspeople responded negatively. They thought it was terrible that such a good teacher was staying with such an evil man. Zacchaeus repented, repaid those he had cheated, and gave money to the poor. Jesus said, "Today salvation has come to this house, since he also is a son of Abraham. For the Son of man came to seek and to save the lost" (Luke 19:1–10).

Archaeological Work

At the Old Testament mound, nearly forty-five feet of current debris represents twenty successive levels of Jericho before the time of Joshua. Ernest Sellin and Carl Watzinger in 1907–1911 excavated the topmost layers of Old Testament Jericho before any accurate way of dating pottery had been established. John Garstang dug from 1929 to 1936, followed by Kathleen Kenyon from 1952 to 1961. It is generally held that today there are no remains at Jericho from the time of Joshua through the days of the judges and kings of Israel. Archaeologist James O. Kelso has written, "One of the major tragedies of Palestinian archaeology is that the Germans excavated Jericho when archaeology was still an infant science." The work of the Germans, along with the erosion caused by wind and rain over the centuries, has apparently prevented positive identification of any archaeological evidence dating from Joshua's conquest. Miss Kenyon's excavations have found evidence that the city existed in the eighth millennium B.C. Thus it is one of the oldest cities in the world.

The Roman road from Jericho to Jerusalem survives in places and a few of its milestones have been found.

REVIEW

1. Briefly describe the modern site of Mount Sinai.
2. Describe the Sinai area. What would have been your feelings had you been one of the Israelites who left Egypt to travel in this area?
3. What happened to the forests, grasses and resources found in Palestine in earlier times? How is the situation changing?
4. What is the biblical significance of Hebron?
5. Why was Jericho located where it was? Describe modern Jericho.
6. What is a "tell"? Why are tells valuable?

CHAPTER TWO
From David to the Exile

Roman Forum built by Herod the Great at Samaria. 2.1

Samaria
Batsell Barrett Baxter

Background Reading: *1 Kings 16:21–34; Micah 1:1–7*

The city of Samaria is located on a hilltop twenty-five miles from the Mediterranean Sea and forty-two miles north of Jerusalem. The site is six-and-one-half miles northwest of Shechem, the first capital of the

northern kingdom of Israel. The Mediterranean Sea is visible from the site.

The name *Samaria* is explained in 1 Kings 16:24 as derived form Shemer, the name of the former owner of the land. The Hebrew word means "watch tower." Omri, king of Israel from 885 to 874 B.C., reigned for a total of twelve years, the last six from Samaria. He purchased the hill of Samaria from Shemer for two talents of silver and then began to fortify the hill. Much later Herod named the site Sebaste in honor of Augustus Caesar (Sebaste is the Greek form for Augustus). The hill is surrounded on three sides by fertile valleys and slopes. Omri's decision to build his capital here may have been prompted by the fact that the area is easy to defend, for no enemy can approach undetected. Today, the mound of ancient Samaria is oval and stands about 300 feet high. The spring for the city is about one mile away. The city comprised about twenty acres, large enough to hold the 27,290 people that Sargon deported, and the 40,000 people who were supposed to live in the city of Herod's day.

Samaria is also the name for the entire region, though the boundaries of the region are not defined in the Bible. It is generally considered to include the land occupied by Ephraim and the western portion of the land occupied by Manasseh. It comprises the area north of the road from Jericho to Bethel and south of a line of hills from Mount Carmel to Mount Gilboa, with the Jordan being the boundary on the east and the Mediterranean on the west. The area produced grain, olives, and other fruits. It was a prosperous area and also benefited from trade with Phoenicia. Samaria is mentioned 125 times in the Bible, mostly in the Old Testament. The word *Samaritan* appears three times in the singular and seven times in the plural.

King Ahab ruled Samaria from 874 to 853 B.C. He did much evil in the sight of the Lord, for he married Jezebel of the Sidonians and erected altars to worship Baal and the Asherah (1 Kings 16:29–33). Ahab wanted the vineyard of Naboth in Jezreel, which was visible from his mountaintop palace, but Naboth refused to give it up since it was part of his family inheritance. Jezebel devised a plan whereby Naboth was falsely accused and as a result stoned. Ahab then took Naboth's vineyard. When Elijah the prophet met Ahab "in Samaria" he pronounced doom on the king (1 Kings 21). This incident inflamed the intense rivalry between Elijah and Ahab, which is best represented by the contest between Elijah and the prophets of Baal on Mount Carmel (1 Kings 18).

In prophecy against Israel, Samaria is often used to designate the entire northern kingdom (Isa. 7:9; 10:9; Amos 3:9; 8:14). It was the pride of Samaria that would doom her (Isa. 9:9), along with the graven images (Isa. 10:10) and the prophets of Baal (Jer. 23:13). The Samaritans had oppressed the poor and crushed the needy. Their women had said to their husbands, "Bring, that we may drink" (Amos 4:1). God's anger was kindled against the city, because it was full of wicked deeds (Mic. 1:1, 5, 6). The fall of Samaria was compared to the coming fall of Jerusalem. The sin of Judah was worse than her elder sister at Samaria (Ezek. 16:46). Samaria had not committed half of the sins that Jerusalem had. Better days would come again when men would plant vineyards in the mountains of Samaria and the fortunes of the area would be restored (Ezek. 16:53–55).

There appears to be only one reference to Samaritans in the Old Testament. (2 Kings 17:29) while they appear several times in the New Testament. In the Old Testament reference "Samaritans" designates Israelites who lived in the northern kingdom. The distinctive history of the Samaritans is difficult to write because of a lack of records. The Samaritans trace their beginning back to Adam. Their traditions run parallel with Jewish history until the time of Joshua. At that point, they have Joshua building a sanctuary on Mount Gerizim, which was the center of all Israelite worship. The religious break with the Jews came when Eli built a rival sanctuary at Shiloh. The two groups coexisted peacefully until the Philistines destroyed Shiloh and Saul later persecuted the tribes who descended from Joseph (the Samaritans).

When the Assyrians conquered the land, they deported only a small number of Samaritans. The Samaritans evidently intermarried with foreign peoples imported into their region. Jewish literature of the intertestamental period refers to the Samaritans as "no nation" and as "the foolish people that dwell in Shechem" (Ecclus. 50:25, 26). Negative feelings about the Samaritans are also reflected in Matthew 10:5–7; John 4:9; and 8:48. They are put in a positive light in Luke 10:29–37; 17:11–19. J. A. Montgomery, in writing of the Samaritans, says: "To sum up the witness of the New Testament: the Samaritan appears as an Israelite, but one whose religion is in the condition of ignorance and whose institutions are irregular."

There are five basic points in the Samaritan faith. (1) They considered themselves true worshipers of God. (2) Supreme authority was placed in the Pentateuch; the rest of the Jewish canon was rejected. They did look forward to the Messiah (John 4:25). (3) The text of the Samaritan Pentateuch in Deuteronomy 27:4 reads "Gerizim," not "Ebal," making Mount Gerizim the true place of worship. (4) They exalted Moses and gave him titles that Christians give to Jesus. (5) Circumcision, the Sabbath, kosher law, and a final judgment were part of their theology. Today Samaritans still live in Nablus and Jaffa and number about 355 persons.

Jesus and Samaria

In New Testament times, Samaria comes into the story of Jesus and the disciples prominently. For example, Jesus was in Samaria when he met the woman at the well and talked to her concerning worship (John 4). At another time a lawyer asked Jesus a series of questions to which Jesus responded by telling the story of a certain man traveling from Jerusalem to Jericho who fell among robbers and was left for dead. The hero of the story was a Samaritan (Luke 10:25–37). While passing between Samaria and Galilee on a trip to Jerusalem, Jesus entered a village where he met ten lepers. He healed them all, but only one returned to express his gratitude. Jesus asked, "Was no one found to return and give praise to God except this foreigner?" (Luke 17:18). The grateful leper was a Samaritan.

Just before his ascension Jesus told the apostles that they would be his witnesses in Jerusalem, Judea, and Samaria, as well as to the ends of the earth (Acts 1:8). As the early Christians were scattered from Jerusalem, Philip went to a city of Samaria and preached the gospel with great response. One of the converts was Simon the sorcerer (Acts 8:4–25). On their way from the north to the Jerusalem conference, Paul and Barnabas passed through Samaria. They told the churches there of the conversion of the Gentiles and were received with great joy (Acts 15:3).

Modern archaeology has helped to fill out some of the history of the ancient Samaritans. For example references to Ahab's house of ivory (1 Kings 22:39) and the beds of ivory (Amos 6:4) have been substantiated by the discovery of five hundred fragments of ivory, most of which were inlays from wooden wall panelings and furniture in Ahab's palace. According to Josephus, Herod loved Sebaste and erected a large beautiful temple on the city's summit for the worship of Augustus as a god. This was the same Herod who built the

Solomon's Palace at Megiddo 2.2

Jerusalem temple. The temple in Samaria had a fore-court which was about 240 feet square and was approached by a staircase 92 feet wide. An altar stood at the foot of the stairs and near it has been found a statue of a Roman emperor. A new city wall was installed measuring two miles in length. Herod also built a theater in Samaria. Many columns are still standing in the Roman forum constructed about 30 B.C.

Megiddo

Harold Hazelip

Background Reading: *Judges 1:27, 28; 2 Kings 23:28–30*

The mound identified with Megiddo is 130 to 200 feet above the surrounding Esdraelon Valley and covers an area of fifteen acres. It would be difficult to find a more strategic site than Megiddo. From the top of the mound the entire length of the Esdraelon Valley can be seen. To the east Mount Gilboa and Mount Tabor can be clearly seen. The western part of the Galilean hills is all that keeps the Mediterranean from sight.

The Via Maris, the "Way of the Sea," connected the lands of Egypt and Assyria. After passing along the Palestinian coast through Philistia and the Plain of Sharon, it crossed the Carmel range to Megiddo. Throughout its three-thousand-year history, Megiddo was located at an important intersection, one that brought much conflict and war.

Archaeologists have uncovered nearly twenty-five different layers dated from before 3300 B.C. until 350 B.C., when the city finally fell into ruins. The largest wall ever found at Megiddo was constructed in approximately the twenty-ninth century B.C. with a thickness of twenty-six feet. Made of brick, it is preserved to a height of thirteen feet.

The Israelite Kings

When the Israelites under Joshua invaded the land, they defeated the king of Megiddo (Josh. 12:7, 21), but they were unable to occupy the city at the time (Judg. 1:27) because the Canaanites had superior weapons, including chariots (Josh. 17:16). It is known that Solomon carried on extensive building projects there. The Old Testament says, "And this is the account of the forced labor which King Solomon levied to build the house of the Lord and his own house and the Millo and the wall of Jerusalem and Hazor and Megiddo and Gezer" (1 Kings 9:15).

Upon being anointed king of Israel by a young prophet sent by Elisha, Jehu began a revolution. In about 842 B.C., he attacked Jehoram, the reigning king of Israel, who was recovering from wounds suffered in the battle against Hazael, king of Syria. Jehoram was killed in the attack by Jehu (2 Kings 9:1–26). Ahaziah, king of Judah, had been an ally of Jehoram against Hazael and was visiting with Jehoram at the time of Jehu's attack. He fled with Jehu in pursuit, was shot in his chariot, and died at Megiddo. A chariot took his body to Jerusalem for burial (1 Kings 8:25—9:28).

Josiah began to reign over Judah in 640 B.C. when he was eight years old. In his eighteenth year, he repaired the temple (2 Kings 22:1–7). The book of the law was found and read to the king (2 Kings 22:8–10). The king renewed the covenant with God and began a series of reforms in Judah. The Lord was still not pleased with Judah (2 Kings 23:1–27). Josiah went to fight Pharaoh Neco, king of Egypt, who was on his way to fight the king of Assyria at Carchemish on the Euphrates River. Josiah intercepted Neco at Megiddo. The

Pharaoh sent a message to Josiah, saying, "What have we to do with each other, king of Judah? I am not coming against you this day, but against the house with which I am at war; and God has commanded me to make haste. Cease opposing God, who is with me, lest he destroy you" (2 Chron. 35:21).

Josiah would not turn away, but disguised himself for the battle. Egyptian archers shot Josiah. The wounded king told his servants, "Take me away, for I am badly wounded." He died shortly thereafter. He was carried back to Jerusalem in his chariot and buried.

The Place Called Armageddon

The New Testament mentions Megiddo only once and that in the form of "Armageddon," meaning "mountain of Megiddo." The text reads, "For they are demonic spirits, performing signs, who go abroad to the kings of the whole world, to assemble them for battle on the great day of God the Almighty. ('Lo, I am coming like a thief! Blessed is he who is awake, keeping his garments that he may not go naked and be seen exposed!') And they assembled them at the place which is called in Hebrew Armageddon" (Rev. 16:14–16).

The mention of "battle" and "Megiddo" in the same context calls to mind the several Old Testament battles fought in the general area. These include Deborah and Sisera (Judg. 4–5), Jehu against Ahaziah (2 Kings 9), and Josiah against Pharaoh Neco (2 Kings 23; 2 Chron. 35). Other noteworthy conflicts occurred nearby. For example, the battle between Gideon and the Midianite-Amalekite forces occurred in the Valley of Jezreel (Judg. 6–7), and the contest between the Philistines and Saul in which Saul died occurred on Mount Gilboa (1 Sam. 31).

General Allenby defeated the Turkish army near Megiddo during World War I on September 19, 1918, and received the title of Viscount Allenby of Megiddo.

One of the most interesting experiences the tourist can have today is a walk through the tunnel connected with the water system of Megiddo. Located on the west side of the tell is a shaft some 80 feet deep with steps cut out of the sides. At the bottom of the shaft is a tunnel which runs under the mound to a spring outside the walls. The tunnel, 230 feet long and 10 feet high, provided water to the city in time of siege. The spring was covered to prevent the enemy from detecting its location. The method of quarrying makes it clear that the tunnel was dug by cutting simultaneously from both ends in a manner similar to the Siloam tunnel in Jerusalem. The two passageways were just over three feet off when they met. The water system is dated variously from about 1200 B.C to the time of Ahab (874–853).

REVIEW

1. How did Samaria become distinct from Israel? How does it remain distinctive even today?
2. Would you agree that the differences between the Jews and the Samaritans typify the trouble experienced today in the whole region? How does Christ have the answer to this turmoil?
3. Why was the valley of Megiddo so important? How did Solomon reinforce this city?
4. Briefly describe Megiddo as it is today.
5. Why was Palestine, especially the area around Megiddo, a "popular" battlefield in history? Why does it remain, even today, a place where nations struggle against one another?

CHAPTER THREE

The Land Where Jesus Walked

Qumran, where the Dead Sea Scrolls were discovered,
with the Dead Sea in the distance. 3.1

The Dead Sea—Sodom

Batsell Barrett Baxter

Background Reading: *Genesis 13:1–13; Genesis 19:24, 25; Deuteronomy 29:22–29*

The Dead Sea is called by several different names in the Old Testament. It is called the Salt Sea (Num. 34:3, 12; Deut. 3:17; Josh. 12:3), the Sea of the Arabah (in some of the same passages), and the Eastern Sea (Ezek. 47:18; Joel 2:20; Zech. 14:8). In extrabiblical literature it is also known as the Sea of Sodom, the Sea of As-

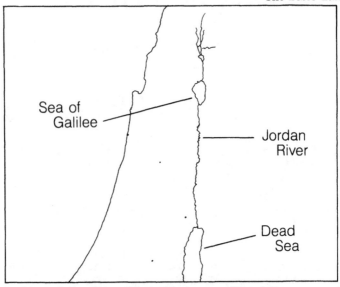

phalt, and the Sea of Lot. The name *Dead Sea* seems to have been introduced into Greek and Latin usage in the second century A.D. The New Testament makes no reference to the sea.

The Geography

The Great Rift is a deep valley stretching from northern Syria through the Valley of Lebanon to the upper Nile Valley and on into southern Africa. The Jordan Valley, the Dead Sea, the Arabah, the Gulf of Aqaba, and the Red Sea occur along the Great Rift. The trough begins at an altitude of 300 feet above sea level in the north and descends to 1,292 feet below sea level at the Dead Sea, the world's lowest point. From the southern end of the Dead Sea the valley floor rises again to a point 750 feet above sea level, a point known as the Arabah, and then slopes down again to the Gulf of Aqaba.

The Dead Sea is fifty-three miles long, nearly eleven miles wide at the widest point, and only two miles wide at the Lisan or "Tongue," which divides the sea into the

34

294-square-mile northern section, which reaches a depth of 1,300 feet, and the 99-square-mile shallow southern basin, which reaches depths of from three to thirty feet. The hills which form the walls of the valley are steep and barren on both sides of the Dead Sea. The mountains on the east rise some 3,000 feet above the water level and are often precipitous. The site of the Machaerus prison, where Herod held John the Baptist and beheaded him, is on the northeast shore of the sea. The hills on the west rise 2,500 feet above the shoreline. Not a single stream enters from the Judean wilderness though two springs feed the sea from the west. One spring is near the Qumran site at the northwest corner of the sea and the other is at En-gedi, where David fled from Saul and found refuge in a cave. The Song of Songs 1:14 speaks of the pleasant vineyards at En-gedi.

Masada, the mountain-top fortress of King Herod where later more than nine hundred zealots committed suicide in A.D. 73 rather than fall into the hands of the Romans, is located on the western shore some 2,000 feet above the water level. The southern part of the sea is very shallow and may once have been a plain on which cities existed. Historians mention the presence of bituminous materials in and about the sea, and chunks still rise to the surface in the southern part today, especially during an earthquake. Southwest of the sea is a five-mile salt ridge covered with clay and limestone. The entire mass is known as Jebel Usdum, the Mount of Sodom.

With barely four inches of rain in a year, the Dead Sea gets its water from the Arnon, Udhemi, Zerqa, Zered, and Jordan Rivers. The Jordan adds the most with some six to seven million tons of water daily; but with the hot and arid climate, often rising to 124° Fahrenheit, evaporation keeps pace with the intake. Since there is no outlet the sea is 25 percent solids (some estimates run as high as 33 percent), at least five times the concentration of the ocean, making it the world's densest large body of water. The principal minerals include magnesium, sodium, calcium, potassium, and magnesium bromide. Since the specific gravity of the water exceeds that of the human body, swimming is a bit like floating a cork. The water is bitter, distasteful, and oily to the touch. It is extremely painful to the eyes, making swimming less than an enjoyable experience. Swimming in the sea requires a bath of fresh water immediately afterwards. All forms of marine life find it impossible to live in the sea, even salt-water varieties.

Mineral extraction is being carried on commercially in the shallow southern end of the sea. This practice dates back to Roman and Arab times. It is estimated today that the sea contains twenty-two billion tons of magnesium chloride, eleven billion tons of common table salt, six billion tons of calcium chloride, two billion tons of potassium chloride, 989 million tons of magnesium bromide, and 200 million tons of gypsum.

The Biblical Story

Sodom, located at the southern end of the Dead Sea, came into the biblical story when Abraham and Lot, while living and grazing their flocks near Bethel, decided that they must separate. Conflicts arose between their herdsmen and Abraham did not want the conflict to continue. He urged Lot to choose where he would like to live, and Lot "lifted up his eyes, and saw that the Jordan valley was well watered everywhere like the garden of the Lord, like the land of Egypt, in the direction of Zoar." And Lot "dwelt among the cities of the valley and moved his tent as far as Sodom" (Gen. 13:2–13).

While Lot was living in Sodom four eastern kings made war on the five kings in the valley and carried away many of the people, including Lot. Hearing that his relative was among those captured, Abraham took 318 men and pursued the retreating army as far as Dan. He attacked by night and rescued Lot's family and possessions (Gen. 14:1–16). When he returned he met Melchizedek, king of Salem and priest of God. Abraham gave to Melchizedek a tenth of the plunder which he had recovered and returned the rest to the king of Sodom, taking only what he and his men had eaten on the way (Gen. 14:17–24).

While Abraham lived at the oaks of Mamre three angels came to his tent, in the form of men. The Lord used them to tell Abraham, "Because the outcry against Sodom and Gomorrah is great and their sin is very grave, I will go down to see whether they have done altogether according to the outcry which has come to me; and if not, I will know" (Gen. 18:20, 21). The men of Sodom were guilty of homosexuality, giving rise to the words *sodomy* and *sodomite* in our language today.

Because of his love for Lot, Abraham pleaded with the Lord not to destroy the city, but since not even ten righteous people could be found in the city God did determine to destroy it. While sitting at the gate of Sodom, Lot was warned by two of the angels of its impending doom and urged to take his family and leave. After some hesitation Lot's family fled to the city of Zoar. "Then the Lord rained on Sodom and Gomorrah brimstone and fire from the Lord out of heaven; and he overthrew those cities, and all the valley, and all the inhabitants of the cities, and what grew on the ground" (Gen. 19:24, 25). Lot's wife looked back as she fled and became a pillar of salt. Abraham watched Sodom and Gomorrah go up like the smoke of a furnace, viewing from a distance at his dwelling place near Hebron.

Symbolic Meaning

Sodom and Gomorrah are mentioned numerous times in the Scriptures. Moses, for example, compared the overthrow of the land whose people disobey God to the overthrow of those two ancient cities. He pointed out that the whole land would become "brimstone and salt, and a burnt-out waste, unsown, and growing nothing, where no grass can sprout" (Deut. 29:23). The prophets compared the overthrow of various countries to the overthrow of Sodom and Gomorrah (Isa. 13:19; Jer. 49:18; Lam. 4:6; Amos 4:11). Jesus mentioned Sodom when the Twelve were sent out on their mission and given instructions on preaching (Matt. 10:1–15); in his sermon against Capernaum, Bethsaida, and Chorazin (Matt. 11:20–24); and in describing his second coming (Luke 17:22–38).

Several sites have been proposed as the location of ancient Sodom and Gomorrah. William Albright and others have suggested that the cities may be under what is now the southern part of the Dead Sea. More recent suggestions connect the cities with several sites east of the southern section of the Dead Sea. Excavations in this area indicate that fire played a major role in the destruction of the cities. Of these excavations, Harry Thomas Frank wrote in the *Biblical Archaeologist* (Dec., 1978): "Moreover, they have suggested that many . . . cities in the south met a sudden and violent end." At Bab edh 'Drah, which lies slightly east of the tongue of the Dead Sea and is 540 feet above the level of the sea, another archaeologist notes there is "evidence of severe burning on many of the stones." In this city, which may date back to the thirty-second century B.C., archaeologists uncovered a structure believed similar to the gate at which Lot was sitting when the angels appeared to him. Seeds collected from the debris in this region indicate that it was once a very prosperous area producing wheat, barley, dates, wild plums, peaches, grapes, figs, pistachio nuts, almonds, olives, pine nuts, lentils, chick peas, pumpkins and watermelon. Flax and castor-oil plants were also raised.

A visit to this arid and desolate crevice in the earth's surface, coupled with the awesome biblical story of God's destruction of ancient Sodom and Gomorrah, leaves one deeply moved. The record of God's righteous indignation against the wickedness of these ancient people still stands in stark relief. One cannot but draw a parallel between the ancient sins and the sins of the modern world and wonder about God's feelings toward the people who inhabit some of the great cities of our own day.

Jordan River as it flows out of the south end of the Sea of Galilee. 3.2

The Jordan River

Batsell Barrett Baxter

Background Reading: *Numbers 26:1–4; Joshua 4:4–7; Matthew 3:4–17; Mark 10:1*

39

Of the world's many great rivers, the Jordan is certainly one of the most famous. While it is neither as large as many of the others, nor as significant in producing power, nor as important for commerce, it has been of great interest to millions of people through thousands of years. The Great Rift, the deepest continental depression on earth, stretches from Syria to Africa. Central to the depression is the Jordan River Valley. The Dead Sea, some fifty-three miles long and eleven miles wide, occupies the deepest part of the rift.

Sources of the Jordan

Four sources found in the watershed of Mount Hermon form the Jordan River. The first stream begins in Banias, named after the pagan god Pan, and issues from a cave as a full-blown river. Beginning at the foot of Mount Hermon some 1,200 feet above sea level it is only six miles long. The Springs of Leddan, about four miles west of Banias, form the second source of the Jordan. The third river begins on the west slopes of Mount Hermon at about 1,700 feet above sea level and is known as the Hasbani. The fourth source is the river Bareighit which contains a beautiful waterfall. With the junction of the four sources the Jordan River flows seven miles before entering into what was formerly Lake Huleh, before it was drained some years ago. Only a marshy area remains today. Reeds, bulrushes, high grass, and papyrus flourish in the area, which is some 230 feet above sea level. The Jordan travels ten more miles to the Sea of Galilee which is 690 feet below sea level, dropping more than 900 feet in that short distance. The Sea of Galilee is about thirteen miles long and eight miles wide at its widest point.

The air distance between the Sea of Galilee and the Dead Sea is only sixty-five miles, but the meandering Jordan travels 135 miles between them. The Jordan drops 600 feet in its trip down the valley, from Galilee's

690 feet below sea level to the Dead Sea's 1292 feet below sea level. The average width of the riverbed is about ninety-eight feet, while the depth ranges from three to ten feet. The valley ranges in width from three to fourteen miles. During flood times, the Jordan swells to a width of one-half mile in certain areas.

The Jordan Valley

As the river approaches the Dead Sea, the Jordan Valley gradually develops into several levels. The lowest level, next to the river, is what the Arabs call the Zor. It has thickets of tamarisk, willow, poplar, cane, and reeds. Scripture calls this "the jungle of the Jordan." It is utterly desolate and nearly impenetrable. This jungle was the habitat of the lion in ancient times but none have been seen in recent years. On either side of the Zor are the Qattarah hills, desolate badlands of ash-gray marl appearing in different shapes and forms. The next level is the Ghor, forming the highest part of the valley. It is often a fertile area. In the area immediately south of the Sea of Galilee there are numerous kibbutzim with lush irrigated fields, fine orchards, and artificial fish ponds.

Several rivers join the Jordan on its trip between the two seas. The Yarmuk joins from the east just a few miles south of Galilee and nearly doubles the size of the Jordan. Near Beth-shan on the west the Jalud (Harod) joins the Jordan. Still later, the Jurm, Yabis, Kufrinjeh, Rajib, and Jabbok enter from the east while the Farah and Qelt join from the west. Nelson Glueck, the archaeologist, found over seventy sites in the valley, indicating a widespread occupation in ancient times, with the more prominent cities being Adam, Succoth, Jabesh-gilead, Pella, Jericho, and Gilgal.

The Jalud River entering near Beth-shan was the river where Gideon had his men drink so that he could determine which ones to choose for his army (Judg.

7:1–8). Even though some six bridges cross the Jordan today (not all are open), the first bridges on the river did not appear until Roman times. Remains of a Roman bridge can be seen at Damiya. There were also some fifty-four fords on the Jordan which were used in ancient times. The Jericho police searched for the Israelite spies all the way to the fords (Josh. 2:7). Jacob crossed the "ford of the Jabbok" (Gen. 32:22) and David crossed the "fords of the wilderness" (2 Sam. 15:28; 17:16, 22).

Biblical Events

The Jordan River is mentioned some 195 times in the Bible with the bulk of the occurrences in the Old Testament. When Abraham suggested that he and Lot separate because of the strife between their herdsmen, Lot "saw that the Jordan valley was well watered everywhere" (Gen. 13:10) and so chose that area. It was at the Jabbok that Jacob wrestled with the angel (Gen. 32:22–31). The Israelites, waiting to enter the Promised Land, "encamped in the plains of Moab beyond the Jordan at Jericho" (Num. 22:1). The tribes were numbered as they camped by the Jordan (Num. 26) and not a man who had left Egypt was counted except for Moses, Joshua, and Caleb (vv. 63–65).

The Book of Joshua opens with God's command to Joshua, "Moses my servant is dead; now therefore arise, go over this Jordan, you and all this people, into the land which I am giving to them" (Josh. 1:2). When the people were prepared, the priests led the way across the Jordan, carrying the ark of the covenant. As they dipped their feet into the water, the water stopped flowing "and rose up in a heap far off, at Adam . . . and the people passed over opposite Jericho" (Josh. 3:16). Joshua ordered each of twelve men to take a stone out of the Jordan and set it up as a memorial. When the people had passed, the priests who were standing in the Jordan and holding the ark of the covenant came out of the dry river and the waters returned (Josh. 4:1–18). The stones were set up at Gilgal (Josh. 4:19–24).

Before crossing the Jordan and dwelling near the brook Cherith where he was fed by the ravens, Elijah warned Ahab about the coming drought (1 Kings 17:1–7). Leaving Jericho, Elijah and Elisha came to the Jordan. "Then Elijah took his mantle, and rolled it up, and struck the water, and the water was parted to the one side and to the other, till the two of them could go over on dry ground" (2 Kings 2:8). On the other side, Elisha asked Elijah for a double measure of his spirit and witnessed as a chariot and horses of fire took the old prophet into the whirlwind and on into heaven. Taking his companion's mantle, Elisha went back to the Jordan and parted the river to walk across (2 Kings 2:9–14). A Syrian named Naaman came to Elisha to be healed of his leprosy. The prophet directed him to wash seven times in the Jordan River and promised that he would then be clean (2 Kings 5:1–14).

Jesus' Baptism

John the Baptist preached in the wilderness of Judea and baptized in the river Jordan (Matt. 3:5, 6; Mark 1:5; Luke 3:3; John 1:28). Jesus came from Galilee from the city of Nazareth and requested that John baptize him in the Jordan River. After the immersion of Jesus, the Spirit of God descended upon Jesus and a voice from heaven spoke, saying, "This is my beloved Son, with whom I am well pleased" (Matt. 3:13–17; Mark 1:9–11; Luke 3:21–23). At least seven sites along the Jordan have been claimed as the location where Jesus was baptized; however, it cannot be known with certainty where that important event took place. John 3:23 indicates that John was baptizing at Aenon near

Salim. The name *Aenon* means springs, though it is not known exactly which springs.

Jesus was often in the area of the Jordan during his public ministry. When he was at Jericho and at Caesarea Philippi, he was near the Jordan and may have crossed it on those trips. On his trips from Galilee to Jerusalem, if he bypassed ancient Samaria as many did, he may very well have traveled down the Jordan Valley (Matt. 19:1; Mark 10:1).

Archaeologists have added interesting information concerning the history of the Jordan. For example, skeletal remains of elephants and rhinoceroses have been found near Lake Huleh, while Kathleen Kenyon has shown that Jericho is one of the oldest cities in the world, claiming that she has found evidence that dates it to the eighth millennium B.C.

Sea of Galilee 3.3

where Jesus is known to have lived and worked, stirs the emotions of the traveler deeply. The Jordan has been mentioned prominently in sermons and also in songs. Among the latter are such songs as "On Jordan's Stormy Banks," "Jordan River, I'm Bound to Cross," and "There Is a Sea Which Day by Day." The Jordan has also been used to illustrate the life of a human being. Beginning small and fresh, it moves with great haste ultimately to bitterness and death. It has also been used as a figure of death, "passing over Jordan" suggesting the end of this earthly life and entrance into the life to come. All in all, it has been one of the most significant rivers in all history.

The Sea of Galilee
Batsell Barrett Baxter

Background Reading: *Luke 5:1–11; Matthew 15:29–32; Matthew 14:22–36*

One of the most beautiful and most appealing bodies of water in the world is the Sea of Galilee. The earliest name for this freshwater lake was Chinnereth, a name which dates back to the fifteenth century B.C. The name is thought to mean "harp" and was probably chosen because the lake is harp-shaped or pear-shaped. Later the name *Gennesaret* was applied to the lake (Luke 5:1), and the New Testament also calls this body of water the Sea of Tiberias (John 6:1; 21:1). The best-known name, however, is the Sea of Galilee, a word which means "ring" or "circle."

The Sea of Galilee is 690 feet below sea level, thirteen miles long, eight miles at its widest, and some thirty-two miles in circumference. The greatest depth is about 170 feet. The lake is supplied by springs, but the majority of its water comes from the Jordan River, which enters on the north and leaves on the south. The waters are collected from Mount Hermon and flow through the Huleh marsh before reaching Galilee.

The Sea of Galilee is about sixty miles north of Jerusalem. The mountains of Galilee rise to the northwest to heights of about 4,000 feet above sea level while the hills immediately to the east and west of the lake rise 1,500 to 2,000 feet above sea level. This means that the drop from the heights to the lake surface is over 2,600 feet in some places. Several hot mineral springs are found on the southwest shore of the lake.

Concerning Galilee, Josephus wrote, "The land is everywhere so rich in soil and pasturage and produces such variety of trees that even the most indolent are tempted by these facilities to devote themselves to agriculture." Wheat, barley, figs, grapes, pomegranates, olives, and numerous vegetables grow well in the area because of the hot climate and the abundant water. The region around Galilee was known for its agriculture, dyeing, tanning, boat-building, fishing, and curing of fish. Over forty different kinds of fish are found in the Sea of Galilee.

Some maintain that in New Testament times, no fewer than nine cities grew up on the shore of the lake, each with a population of at least fifteen thousand. Ruins of palaces, hippodromes, theaters, and baths built by the Greeks and Romans also testify to the ample population in ancient times. During our visit, on a beautiful cloudless evening we were able to stand on the porch of the Chinnereth Hotel, which extends to the water's edge, and to observe the lights of fifteen different villages clustered about the lake. None of these, however, has a population even approaching fifteen thousand.

Situated in a deep valley protected on the east and west by high mountains, the lake is a likely place for storms. The cool air masses from the mountain heights rush down the steep slopes to the surface of the lake, causing the waters of the lake to erupt with sudden violent force. Such tempests are not infrequent and are extremely dangerous to small craft.

Christ and Galilee

The word *Galilee* appears in the Bible a total of seventy-three times, sometimes referring to the region and at other times to the lake. The Old Testament is virtually silent about the sea; but as a result of Jesus' moving his ministry to Capernaum after leaving Nazareth, the Sea of Galilee is very prominently mentioned in the New Testament.

When walking along the edge of the sea on one occasion, Jesus saw Peter, Andrew, James, and John mending their nets after a night of unsuccessful fishing. He borrowed one of the boats and from it preached a sermon to the people who stood or sat upon the sloping bank of the sea. Afterward, he called these men to be full-time disciples. They left their boats and followed him (Luke 5:1–11).

It was on one of the mountains overlooking the sea that Jesus preached the Sermon on the Mount (Matt. 5–7). It was around the shore of the sea that he presented his several parables concerning the kingdom of heaven (Matt. 13). Much of Christ's most meaningful teaching was done in his many travels about the Sea of Galilee.

Some ten of the thirty-three recorded miracles of Jesus took place around this beautiful body of water. On its shores he fed the five thousand (Matt. 14:13–23; Mark 6:30–46; Luke 9:10–17; John 6:1–15). At a later time he fed the four thousand (Matt. 15:32–39; Mark 8:1–9). At another time, when the disciples had rowed some three or four miles and the sea became very violent, Jesus walked upon the sea to them and then stilled the tempest (Matt. 14:22–36; Mark 6:47–56;

John 6:16–21). Jesus also healed many who were ill, including Peter's wife's mother, the man with palsy who was let down through the roof of the house, and others who were deaf, blind, and lame.

It was also in this same area that Jesus sifted the multitude, offering them spiritual bread rather than the loaves and the fishes which they sought, ultimately finding that the multitudes turned away, leaving only the apostles with him (John 6). After his death and resurrection Jesus again visited the Sea of Galilee; he appeared one morning to seven of his disciples and prepared for them a breakfast of fish (John 21).

Herod and the Jews

Until his death in 4 B.C., Herod the Great, as king of Judea and governor of Galilee, ruled the territory which included the Sea of Galilee. His son Antipas took that part of his father's domain which included the sea and moved his capital to Tiberias. Antipas ruled the area during the entire life of Jesus, except for the first few years. When the Jews were expelled from Jerusalem in A.D. 70, the center of Jewish scholarship was transferred to Galilee. The Mishnah and the Talmud were later produced in Tiberias. The area was the home of the Masoretes, who worked on the Old Testament text. The Sanhedrin also was transferred to Tiberias.

Tiberias is mentioned only in John 6:23, where it is described as a place where boats following Jesus came from. The city was named in honor of Tiberius Caesar (A.D. 14–37) and was built by Herod Antipas (4 B.C.–A.D. 39). The city is located about five miles northwest of the place where the Jordan flows out of the Sea of Galilee. Herod's city included a stadium, and other Roman buildings constructed over ancient tombs. Some scholars suggest that the city had no Jewish population, but the presence of a place of prayer and the later prevalence of Jews in the area may suggest that Jews lived in the city at the time of Jesus. The tombs of Maimonides (twelfth-century Spanish-Jewish scholar) and of Rabbi Akiva (second-century scholar) are in the area. About three miles north of Tiberias is the site of Migdal, the ancient Magdala, the home village of Mary Magdalene.

Bethsaida is located on the northern shore of the lake. The word means "house of the fisher" or "house of the hunter." Bethsaida is called a city in Luke 9:20 and John 1:44, and a village in Mark 8:26. Philip, Andrew, and Peter were from Bethsaida though Peter had a house in Capernaum also (Matt. 8:14).

Altogether, the Sea of Galilee is one of the most rewarding experiences in a visit to Israel. We could be very sure that we were in the exact area where Jesus lived and worked. Cities change, but lakes and mountains remain much the same through the centuries. As we read again many of the familiar Scriptures concerning Christ's life and work, we felt very near to the Lord. Fishing is still a major activity on the sea and is done in much the same way as it was done in New Testament times.

REVIEW

1. What are the three distinct geographical regions that make up Palestine?
2. How does the Jordan Valley provide a natural border and barrier between Israel and its neighbors?
3. Describe the Dead Sea and the surrounding area.
4. Where do scholars think Sodom was located?
5. Describe Masada. Why was it built? Why is it so meaningful to the Jews today?
6. As Jesus went through the land, why would He be reminded of the king who tried to kill Him as a child?
7. Why are storms likely on the Sea of Galilee? Describe the area around the sea.
8. Why was the Sea of Galilee so significant in the New Testament and yet hardly mentioned in the Old Testament?

CHAPTER FOUR
The Land of Galilee

Traditional Mount of the Beatitudes, where the Sermon on the Mount was preached, overlooks the north end of the Sea of Galilee. 4.1

Mount of Beatitudes
Harold Hazelip

Background Reading: *Luke 6:12, 13; Matthew 5:1–12; Matthew 6:25–34*

The road from Tiberias to Metula skirts the northwest corner of the Sea of Galilee. The road branches at Tabgha. A church building known as the Church of the Loaves and Fishes appears to have been erected here in the fourth century. It is thought to be the site of the miracle of the feeding of the five thousand (Matt. 14:19–21).

51

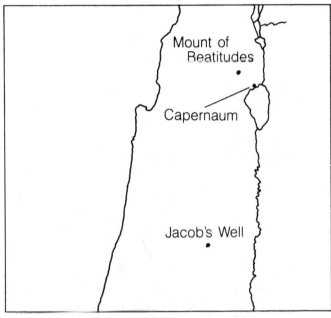

Nearby is the Chapel of the Primacy, erected in 1943 by the Franciscans to mark the "Feed my sheep" episode of John 21:15–17. Capernaum is two miles further down the road.

Across the road from the Chapel of the Primacy, about two-and-one-half miles northeast of Tabgha, is a hill which rises some 330 feet above the sea (which is itself 690 feet below sea level). This hill is known as the Mount of Beatitudes. A round chapel was built atop the hill in 1937. Tradition indicates that Jesus presented the Sermon on the Mount here (Matt. 5–7) and that it was on this same hillside that he called his apostles. Luke records: "In these days he went out into the hills to pray; and all night he continued in prayer to God. And when it was day, he called his disciples, and chose from them twelve, whom he named apostles" (Luke 6:12, 13).

Archaeological explorations show that the Mount of Beatitudes was uninhabited until the Byzantine period. The implication is that Jesus would have found the mountain, with its numerous scattered rocks, available for his speeches to the large crowds.

From the Mount of Beatitudes one's panoramic view extends from the second-century synagogue at Capernaum to the city of Tiberias on the hillside west of the Sea of Galilee. The Church of the Beatitudes is entered through a lovely garden of olives, cacti, and palms, and is built on a foundation of basalt. It is unusual because of its white dome which is surrounded by a colonnade of marble columns. The windows are stained glass, depicting scenes from the life of Jesus, while the walls contain quotations from the Sermon on the Mount. The shrine is octagonal in shape. This commemorates the eight Beatitudes, one of which is inscribed on each of the windows. Symbols of the seven virtues (justice, charity, prudence, faith, fortitude, hope, temperance) are represented in the pavement around the altar.

A visit to this peaceful site helps one to understand the source of a number of Jesus' illustrations. The soft slopes carpeted in springtime with flowers call to mind the lilies of the field (Matt. 6:28). The active bird life recalls the "birds of the air" (Matt. 6:26). A number of cities visible from the mount almost seem to be "set on a hill" (Matt. 5:14).

Bolt, Beranek, and Newman, Incorporated, of Cambridge, Massachusetts, the same firm which analyzed the 18½-minute gap in the key Watergate tape and experimented with rifle shots at the site of the John Kennedy assassination in Dallas, has also participated in a study of the acoustics and crowd capacity of natural theaters in Palestine. One of the test sites was the cove near Capernaum where the road is about three hundred feet from the shoreline.

The specialists determined that speaking from the center of the cove, (i.e., from about thirty feet off the shore) would provide the best situation for clear communication. One of the experimenters suggested: "It is not unlikely that Jesus and other orators of his day were aware of these aspects of speech in an amphitheater. Thus, it is possible that he chose this particular site and sat in the boat away from the sloping audience for these reasons. There is no denying that speech communication would have been quite good inside this bowl."

The experimenters also suggested that as many as seven thousand people could have assembled in this sloping area next to the sea and have clearly heard a human voice originating from the center of the cove. The bowllike shape of the area would permit the speaker to be seen from almost any angle. It is entirely conceivable that the "great crowds" which the Gospel states that Jesus spoke to could have gathered here.

Synagogue at Capernaum.   4.2

Capernaum
Harold Hazelip

Background Reading: *Matthew 4:12–17; Matthew 8:5–17; Mark 1:21–28*

Although Capernaum is derived from the Aramaic *Kepar Nahum,* which means "village of Nahum," there is no proof of any relationship between this spot and the Old Testament prophet Nahum. Located on the northern shore of the Sea of Galilee, the city lies along the coast on a narrow plain with ruins covering a strip nearly a mile long. It is located some two-and-one-half miles from the point where the Jordan River enters the Sea of Galilee.

Jesus' Home Town

Capernaum is mentioned some sixteen times in the Bible, all in the Gospels. The city is first mentioned after Jesus' temptation in the wilderness; hearing that John had been arrested, Jesus left Nazareth and moved to Capernaum. The text mentions that Capernaum is by the sea and in the territory of Zebulun and Naphtali (Matt. 4:12, 13).

We are not told why Jesus, early in his ministry, left Nazareth for Capernaum. It is the only place in the Gospels where Jesus is described as being "at home" (Mark 2:1). Following the miracle at Cana and before the cleansing of the temple, Jesus, his family, and his disciples went to Capernaum to stay for a few days (John 2:12).

Some have speculated that Jesus moved his residence to the seaside city because it was larger or because several of his disciples had their homes there. It was near this place that he called the fishermen (Simon and Andrew, James and John—Matt. 4:18–22) and the tax-collector (Matthew was sitting in the Capernaum tax office—Matt. 9:9). Matthew invited the tax-collectors along with Jesus and his disciples to dinner (Matt. 9:10–13).

Biblical Events

The centurion of Capernaum asked that Jesus heal his paralyzed servant without coming to his home. Jesus did so, being amazed that the centurion had the kind of faith that he had been looking for among the Jews (Matt. 8:5–13).

On one occasion when Jesus was returning from Jerusalem, he healed the son of a nobleman in Capernaum. The dying son was healed immediately as Jesus spoke, without requiring his physical presence. It was the seventh hour when Jesus told the nobleman that his son was healed; the man's servants later confirmed that it was the same hour that the boy began to mend. This is called the second sign after Jesus came from Judea to Galilee (John 4:46–54).

Jesus preached one sermon in which he was very critical of the cities which had refused to repent at his preaching. He included Bethsaida, Chorazin, and Capernaum. He compared his "home" to Sodom, saying that if the mighty works done in Capernaum had been done in Sodom, it would still be around. He indicated that Capernaum would be brought down to Hades and that Sodom would have a better chance in judgment (Matt. 11:23, 24).

It was also at Capernaum that Jesus went to Peter's house and healed his mother-in-law, who was sick with a fever. He touched her hand and the fever went away (Matt. 8:14–17; Mark 1:29–31). It may have been just outside this house that Jesus healed many others that evening, fulfilling the words of Isaiah, "He took our infirmities and bore our diseases" (Isa. 53:4).

Early in his ministry, Jesus was teaching in the synagogue at Capernaum on the Sabbath when a man with an unclean spirit challenged him. Jesus rebuked him and took the spirit out of the man. The people were impressed with his authority (Mark 1:21–28).

A bit later, Jesus crossed the Sea of Galilee and then returned to Capernaum. The people filled the house where he was, listening to him. A paralytic, carried by four men, sought access to Jesus. When they saw the crowd, they made an opening in the roof and lowered the man into Jesus' presence. Jesus forgave his sins. Then, to establish his power with the questioning scribes, he healed the man, who took up his pallet and walked away. It was in this house in Capernaum that the people said, "We never saw anything like this," and, "We have seen strange things today" (Mark 2:12; Luke 5:26).

Jesus was speaking to a crowd in Capernaum when a ruler of the synagogue named Jairus appealed to Jesus to lay his hand on his dying daughter. As Jesus was working his way through the crowded streets of the city, a woman with a bleeding problem which had afflicted her for twelve years, seeking to be healed, touched his garment, Jesus felt power leaving him and sought her out to note that a miracle had been performed.

After meeting Jairus' servants, who said the girl was already dead, Jesus continued to the ruler's house, where he saw flute players and a noisy crowd. He told them the twelve-year-old girl was not dead but sleeping. While they laughed, Jesus put the mob outside and raised the girl with the words, "Talitha cumi" (Mark 5:41). Jesus told those present to tell no one what had happened.

After feeding the five thousand, Jesus' disciples boarded the boat for the trip to Capernaum, only to run into a storm. Jesus walked the three or four miles across the sea to their boat, frightening them in the process. They took him into the boat and the boat was immediately at land (John 6:16–21). The people who had been fed on the other side of the sea, not able to find Jesus, got into boats the next day and headed toward Capernaum. They finally found Jesus at Capernaum and asked how he happened to be there. Jesus accused them of following him because of the free food. He then delivered his discourse on the bread of life: "I am the bread of life; he who comes to me shall not hunger, and he who believes in me shall never thirst" (John 6:22–40).

Following his transfiguration, as Jesus and his disciples worked their way back from the mountain, the disciples discussed who would be the greatest. Jesus took a child of Capernaum into his arms and began a lecture on humility: "If any one would be first, he must be last of all and servant of all" (Mark 9:33–37).

Also after Jesus' return to Capernaum following the transfiguration, the tax-collectors approached Peter about the tax which Jesus owed. Peter asked Jesus about it and a discussion followed. Jesus told Peter to take his equipment and catch a fish. In its mouth would be a coin which would pay the tax for both of them. Today a delicious fish called "St. Peter's fish" is served in restaurants near the Sea of Galilee. It is so named because of its wide mouth, giving rise to the tradition that it is the kind of fish Peter caught before paying the taxes (Matt. 17:24–27).

Remains at Capernaum

The synagogue ruins are the most interesting remains for visitors to Capernaum today. The longer archaeologists investigate Capernaum, the more recent the date attached to its synagogue. It was originally dated to the first century A.D. by Charles Wilson in 1806, but the date was later moved to the second century by H. H. Kitchener, and later to the third century.

Several scholars today favor a fourth-century date, though not without argument. It is possible that the present synagogue rests on the remains of the synagogue which the centurion built (Luke 7:5) and in which Jesus taught.

Extensive house building occurred in Capernaum in the first century B.C. The residential area was built in eighty-foot squares. In each square were several houses complete with courtyards. The unroofed courtyards had grinding stones, outdoor ovens, and stairways leading to the flat roofs. Fish hooks found beneath the floors suggest that this was a fishing village.

Josephus, the Jewish historian, records that he was hurt near the Jordan while on a military activity: "The horse on which I rode, and upon whose back I fought,

Mt. Gerezim, where the Samaritans still offer sacrifices on the Passover, as seen from Jacob's Well. 4.3

fell into a quagmire, and threw me to the ground, and I was bruised on my wrist, and carried into a village named Cepharnome, or Capernaum." He also writes a flattering description of the area around Capernaum as a place whose "nature is wonderful as well as its beauty," whose "soil is so fruitful that all sorts of trees can grow upon it."

The shore of the Sea of Galilee has a small inlet for boats at Capernaum, making this a pleasant place to relive biblical events.

Jacob's Well

Harold Hazelip

Background Reading: *Genesis 12:6, 7; Joshua 24:32; John 4:7–38*

Leaving Judea, on his way to Galilee, Jesus passed through the district of Samaria and came near the city of Sychar. He sat down at Jacob's well to rest. Jesus' disciples had gone into the city, which was not far away (John 4:8). A woman of Samaria came to the well for water and fell into conversation with him. She mentioned that the well was deep and alluded to Mount Gerizim where her fathers worshiped.

From Jerome (fourth century) on there is mention of a church building on the spot with the historic well inside. The building was apparently damaged in the Samaritan revolts (A.D. 484 and 529) and restored by the emperor Justinian (A.D. 527–565). The Crusaders recorded the construction of a new building, which fell in A.D. 1187 to the Muslims. The Greek Orthodox acquired the spot in 1860. Work on a church building was begun in 1914 but has never been finished.

The Greek monk in charge of the site will let down a pail to show the depth of the well, which would be about fifty-eight feet if cleared of rubbish. The water is good and fresh in contrast to the bitter water from the abundant springs at the foot of nearby Mount Gerizim.

About 540 feet north of the well is Joseph's tomb, marked by a white dome. It was restored in 1868 and is accepted by Jews, Samaritans, Muslims, and Christians alike.

Old Testament Shechem

The name *Sychar* (John 4) does not appear elsewhere in Scripture. It has traditionally been identified with Shechem. However, excavations at Shechem indicate the area was not occupied in New Testament times, and archaeologists today tend to identify Sychar with El Askar, on the eastern slope of Mount Ebal, about a half mile north of Jacob's well.

Shechem is located about forty miles north of Jerusalem in the pass between Mount Gerizim and Mount Ebal. The main east-west and north-south roads converge here. The word *Shechem* seems to mean "shoulder" or "slope." A good water supply and a fertile plain east of the city combined to make the city wealthy and powerful.

Obeying God's command to move, Abraham came to Shechem, to the oak of Moreh, and built an altar. Before Abraham moved to the Bethel area, God said to him, "To your descendants I will give this land" (Gen. 12:7).

Jacob returned to Palestine following his marriages and the beginning of his family. After the meeting with Esau, the text states, "And Jacob came safely to the city of Shechem, which is in the land of Canaan, on his way from Paddan-aram; and he camped before the city. And from the sons of Hamor, Shechem's father, he bought for a hundred pieces of money the piece of land on which he had pitched his tent. There he erected an altar and called it El-Elohe-Israel" (Gen. 33:18–20).

Jacob's sons were pasturing their sheep near Shechem when Joseph was sent to check on them. Not finding them there he went to Dothan on the advice of a local man he had met wandering in the field around Shechem (Gen. 37:12–17). Later, Joseph's body was brought along on the exodus from Egypt and buried at Shechem when the people conquered the land (Josh. 24:32).

When the land was divided among the tribes, the boundary between Ephraim and Manasseh passed near Shechem. Shechem also served as a city of refuge (Josh. 17:7; 20:7).

Joshua called an assembly of the tribes at Shechem following successes in the conquest of Canaan (Josh. 24:1). It was at Shechem that Joshua challenged the people with his last message: "And if you be unwilling to serve the Lord, choose this day whom you will serve, whether the gods your fathers served in the region beyond the River, or the gods of the Amorites in whose land you dwell; but as for me and my house, we will serve the Lord" (Josh. 24:15, 16).

After Solomon died, his son Rehoboam went to Shechem where the people had gathered to make him king. Jeroboam, hearing of Solomon's death, returned from Egypt and represented the people before Rehoboam. The people requested relief from the heavy burdens Solomon had placed on them. In return, they would be loyal to Rehoboam as king. Rehoboam rejected the advice of the older men and followed the counsel of his younger aides by continuing the burden.

The people refused to follow Rehoboam and his oppressive policy and quickly stoned Adoram, Rehoboam's taskmaster. Jeroboam was then made king of the ten northern tribes, leaving Rehoboam to flee Shechem for Jerusalem. Jeroboam rebuilt Shechem and then moved his capital to Penuel and later to Tirzah (1 Kings 12).

Mounts Gerizim and Ebal

Gerizim and Ebal were the mountains on whose slopes the tribes of Israel assembled under Joshua, fulfilling Moses' command by hearing the curses and the blessings connected with the law. Gerizim was the mount of blessing, Ebal the mount of cursing (Deut. 11:29; 27:11–13; Josh. 8:33, 34). Simeon, Levi, Judah, Issachar, Joseph, and Benjamin were to stand on Mount Gerizim for the blessings; the other six tribes were to stand on Mount Ebal for the curses.

Gerizim is known in Arabic as Jebel et Tor, "the holy mountain." It rises some 2,849 feet above sea level. With Mount Ebal it commanded the entrance to the narrow valley of Shechem. Since this pass gave the only access from east to west into the mountains of Ephraim, and was situated on the main road from the north to the south, it was of strategic importance.

Mount Gerizim has been the spiritual and visible center of Samaritan worship since the beginning of the schism when the Jews returned from Babylonian captivity. The Samaritans erected a rival temple on Mount Gerizim where they continue to celebrate the Passover feast. The whole congregation (only about three hundred Samaritans are left) ascends the mount and spends an entire week there. The site of the celebration is a small trench about eight feet in length which they call the altar. They slaughter the seven Passover lambs there. Close to the altar is a pit which is used as the oven where the sacrifices are burned. The Samaritans also claim that twelve nearby rocks are the ones Joshua set up.

Mount Ebal, located north of and directly opposite Mount Gerizim, is 3,080 feet high. Nineteenth-century travelers frequently praised the view from Mount Ebal.

Modern Nablus

Some have thought that Old Testament Shechem is under the modern city of Nablus, but the results of excavations tend to disprove this. Nablus is the home of some ninety thousand people today and the headquarters of the Samaritans. The city was built in A.D. 72 by Titus, the Roman general. The small remnant of Samaritans, persecuted over the years, still live in Nablus and in a small community near Tel Aviv. In the Samaritan section, on the west side of Nablus, an ancient Pentateuch scroll is shown, which is the only Scripture accepted by the sect. Despite their claims for its antiquity, it dates no earlier than the tenth or eleventh century A.D.

REVIEW

1. What is Qumran? What is the importance of the Dead Sea Scrolls? Where were they found, and how were they discovered?
2. Does Jacob's well still have significance today? Why?
3. Where was Jesus transfigured?
4. What is the real value of archaeology? How is it done?
5. Why is Capernaum biblically significant?
6. What has been found at Capernaum?
7. How was it possible for Jesus to be heard by so many people on the Mount of the Beatitudes?
8. What is located on and around the Mount of Beatitudes today?

CHAPTER FIVE

The Jerusalem Jesus Knew

The Dome of the Rock stands of the temple mountain in Old Jerusalem, where the temple stood in Jesus' day.   5.1

Jerusalem

Batsell Barrett Baxter

Background Reading: *Luke 2:41–50; John 2:13–17; 3:1–21; Acts 1:9–14; Acts 2:1–8*

The word *Jerusalem* is used over eight hundred times in the Bible. This suggests the great importance of the city in biblical history. It is called Urushalim or Urusalim in ancient Egyptian texts, and Salem or Jebus in certain Old Testament passages. Other names applied to the city are Moriah, Zion, City of David, and Ariel. The word *Jerusalem* probably means "founda-

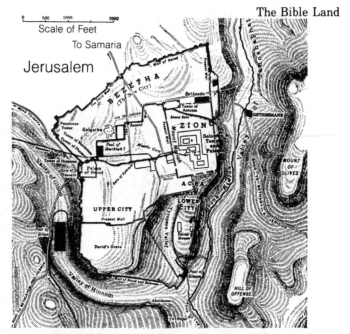

tion of Shalem," though traditionally it is taken to mean "city of peace."

Jerusalem is located thirty-three miles east of the Mediterranean Sea and fourteen miles west of the Dead Sea at an elevation of 2,500 feet. It sits on top of a ridge which reaches from Mount Gilboa in the north to Hebron in the south. It enjoys a protected location and is on the major north-south highway in central Israel.

Hills and Valleys

Jerusalem consists of five once sharply distinguished hills separated by valleys. Erosion and building have altered the hills, while debris and sediment have filled the valleys. On the west and south is the Valley of Hinnom and on the east the Kidron Valley, also known as the King's Valley. The interior of the city was divided by a ravine called the Tyropoeon (cheesemaker's) Valley, which ran from the present

Damascus Gate through the city and out the Dung Gate, passing the Wailing Wall in the process.

Between the Tyropoeon and Kidron Valleys lie three mountains. The southernmost was called Ophel and was the lowest with an elevation of only 2,000 feet. It was the site of the earliest city and because of its sharp drop into the valleys was the easiest to defend. Just north across what was once a slight depression is Mount Moriah. It was originally a threshing floor but was designated by David as the place of sacrifice. It was the site of the three Jewish temples and now holds the Dome of the Rock. The third hill is Mount Bezetha just to the north of the temple area. Herod expanded the temple platform northward and covered the ravine which once separated Moriah from Bezetha.

Between the Tyropoeon and Hinnom Valleys lie two mountains. To the south is Zion, the highest of the five on which Jerusalem was built. A smaller hill or spur occupies the section north of Zion. Jerusalem was not taken by Israel during the conquest, but was later conquered by David, who made it his city. It was to this city that the exiles returned. Jesus often visited the city and the early church was very strong in Jerusalem.

Old Testament History

Archaeological finds date the beginning of Jerusalem in the fourth millennium B.C. or earlier, with a walled city during the Early and Middle Bronze periods (3150–1550). Abraham is connected with the city twice, once when he visited Melchizedek of Salem in Genesis 14 and again when he prepared to offer his son Isaac in the land of Moriah. Perhaps it should be mentioned that neither of these events is assigned by all scholars to Jerusalem. Joshua fought with and slew Adoni-zedek, king of Jerusalem, but did not take the city (Josh. 10). During the period of the judges, the city is mentioned only in passing; it was held by the Jebusites (Judg. 19:10–12).

After being anointed king over all Israel, and after reigning in Hebron for seven-and-one-half years, David took the city of Jerusalem, making it his capital. David accomplished this by challenging several of his strongest military men to take the city, promising the captaincy of his army to the one who was successful. Joab led the way, probably entering the city through the Jebusite shaft—the channel through which a spring outside the northern wall flowed into the city.

David built a palace and the Millo. 2 Samuel 5:9 reads, "And David built the city round about from the Millo inward." The word *Millo* comes from the Semitic root which means "filling." This suggests to some the filling of the ravine separating Mount Ophel from Mount Moriah. Kathleen Kenyon, as a result of excavations, suggested that Millo refers to the rock terraces constructed on the east side of Ophel to provide more room and to fill up the area on the side of the hill which led to the city wall.

David brought the ark to the city and during the years 1003–970 B.C. took concubines and wives who bore him eleven sons (2 Sam. 5–6). It was also here that he committed adultery with Bathsheba and was punished (2 Sam. 11–12). David's son, Absalom, fled from the city but later returned and drove out his father (2 Sam. 13–15). After Absalom's death, David returned to the city and made elaborate preparations for the construction of a temple to God on Mount Moriah, the threshing floor of Araunah the Jebusite (2 Sam. 24; 1 Chron. 21). David died in Jerusalem and was buried there (1 Kings 2).

Solomon followed his father David on the throne and also lived in Jerusalem. Solomon built the temple and an elaborate palace (1 Kings 5–8). The temple construction began in April/May 966 B.C. and was completed in October/November 959 B.C. (1 Kings 6:1, 38). Israel provided the labor for the temple construction but the Phoenicians of Tyre provided the timber (1 Kings 5:6–12; 2 Chron. 2). The construction of the temple forced the expansion of the city walls to the north (cf. 1 Kings 3:1). Solomon's complex presumably included stable facilities (1 Kings 9:19; 10:26), the "House of the Forest of Lebanon" (150 by 75 feet, built on forty-five columns of cedar in three rows), and a large palace (1 Kings 7:2–8). After the completion of his building projects, Solomon hosted the queen of Sheba, took many foreign wives, and built altars to foreign gods (1 Kings 10–11). Solomon ruled Jerusalem for forty years from 970 B.C. to 930. He died and was buried in the city of David.

Hezekiah, who began to reign by himself in 725 B.C., instituted a series of reforms in Jerusalem, including reopening of the temple (2 Chron. 29:3), casting down the pagan altars, and burning the religious paraphernalia that had been brought in by some of his predecessors. During his reign, Hezekiah strengthened the walls of Jerusalem as Sennacherib the Assyrian threatened the city (2 Chron. 32). Hezekiah also diverted the water from Gihon Spring so that the enemy's besieging army would not have access to it. He built a conduit, now known as Hezekiah's tunnel, to bring the water into the city. The ministry of the prophet Isaiah also centered in Jerusalem.

Josiah (640–609 B.C.) was another king who led in reforming the nation after others had carried it into idolatry. Josiah decided to repair the temple and carry out thorough religious reforms. In repairing the temple, he found the book of the law. It was used as a guide for Josiah's work of reform (2 Kings 22–23; 2 Chron. 34–35).

There were four deportations into Babylonian captivity; 605, 597, 586, and 581 B.C. Jerusalem remained the hope of those in exile (Ezek. 34:13; 36:38). Some maintained the practice of praying toward Jerusalem three times each day (Dan. 6:10). Cyrus issued a decree in 538 B.C., authorizing the Jews to return to Jerusalem and to reestablish services at the temple (Ezra 1:2–4). The rebuilding of the temple soon began (Ezra 3–5). A second major return to Jerusalem took place in the summer of 458 B.C. under Ezra (Ezra 7:7). A decade later a third return was led by Nehemiah, who made a nighttime tour of the city just three days after his arrival, then led in the rebuilding of the walls in a period of fifty-two days (Neh. 2, 4–6).

Jesus and Jerusalem

The Roman general Pompey conquered Jerusalem in 63 B.C and made it subject to Rome. Tacitus indicates that Pompey entered the Holy of Holies and was surprised to find it empty. Herod the Great made the right political moves and with the support of Rome ruled Jerusalem from 37 B.C. to 4 B.C. Herod's most famous building project was the temple. Herod extended the temple platform both to the north and south, making the area some 2,500 feet from north to south and 1,000 feet from east to west. Of the temple itself, not a stone remains; but the sacred area today remains much as it was when Herod built it. The famous Wailing Wall on the west and other portions on the east and south sides of the platform can still be seen. Construction of the temple began in 20 B.C. and was not completed until A.D. 64, six years before its destruction in A.D. 70. The date of the statement made to Christ in John 2:20, suggesting that the temple had been under construction for forty-six years, must have been A.D. 27.

Jerusalem figures in the stories of Jesus' birth as the home of Herod (Matt. 2:1–12), the place where Zechariah (the future father of John the Baptist) had

his vision (Luke 1:5–23), and the scene of the presenta-
tion of the infant Jesus at the temple (Luke 2:22–38).
At age twelve, Jesus attended the Passover feast and
stayed behind to speak with the teachers (Luke
2:41–50). After his fast in the wilderness, he was
brought to the pinnacle of the temple where Satan
tempted him to cast himself down (Matt. 4:5–7). John
recorded two trips to Jerusalem for the Passover; during the first of these visits Jesus cleansed the temple
and talked with Nicodemus (John 2:13–22; 3:1–8).
Jesus also journeyed to Jerusalem for the Feast of Tabernacles; on this occasion he taught in the temple, forgave the woman caught in the act of adultery, healed
the man born blind by telling him to wash in the pool of
Siloam, and gave his discourse on the good shepherd
(John 7–10). Jesus was in Jerusalem at other times as
well, and during the last week of his life he was in
Jerusalem daily. He was also there after his resurrection until the time of his ascension from the Mount of
Olives (Luke 24:44–53).

The apostles and others remained in Jerusalem after
Christ's ascension, and were there for the beginning of
the church on Pentecost (Acts 2). Many of the important events connected with the beginning and growth
of the church occurred in Jerusalem, until the members generally were scattered (Acts 8). The apostles remained in Jerusalem.

Archaeological Studies

More than forty-four archaeological enterprises have
been conducted in Jerusalem since 1863, many of
which included several prominent archaeologists. Few
if any other cities in the world have been subjected to
such archaeological scrutiny. The most recent finds
suggest that the ancient city of David probably included about 12 acres. While modern American cities
have about 50 to 80 persons per acre, ancient cities had

closer to 160 people per acre. Given that figure, the population of Davidic Jerusalem was no more than 2,000. Solomon's city included about 32 acres. The estimated population of the walled city of Jerusalem during his reign would be 4,500 to 5,000. In the seventh century B.C. the city is thought to have expanded, adding an additional 125 acres, with the possibility that the population inside the walls then reached 25,000. There are no known archaeological remains of David's city. Very little from the time of Solomon remains and nothing has been found of Solomon's temple except for a pilaster, a rectangular support or pier that was part of a wall.

A line of cemeteries stretching from Akeldama in the south around the east side of Jerusalem has recently been excavated. Most tombs have a central room with niches in which ossuaries (pottery vessels in which the bones are put after a body decays) were placed. Many of these tombs date to the first century A.D. A great deal of excavation and writing has been done trying to locate the walls of the ancient city of Jerusalem. This is extremely difficult since the walls were expanded from time to time, taking in additional territory. The present walls were built by Suleiman II (or Solyman), sultan of Turkey. Known as Suleiman the Magnificent, he lived from 1494 to 1566. At its largest, it is thought that the city comprised about 230 acres. This would mean a possible population of 40,000 people. Josephus, whose figures are generally regarded as unreliable, indicates that the population of Jerusalem at the beginning of the third century B.C. was 120,000 and that 1.1 million Jerusalemites were killed by the Romans in A.D. 70.

The modern visitor to Jerusalem is greatly assisted in his understanding of the ancient city by visiting a model of Jerusalem on the grounds of the Holy Land Hotel. A scaled-down version of Jerusalem as it was in

A.D. 66, some thirty-six years after the time of Jesus, the model is about 95 feet wide and 130 feet long. It represents a city that would have been nearly a mile wide from east to west and a mile-and-a-quarter from north to south. Built under the guidance of the late Michael Avi-Yonah of Hebrew University, the model is revised from time to time as archaeological discoveries are made.

Jerusalem is a city rich in meaning not to just one religious faith, but to three—Jews, Muslims, and Christians. It is extremely difficult to separate facts from traditions. Many of the buildings in Jerusalem could not possibly be authentic, due to the fact that the present-day streets of Jerusalem are in some areas ten or twenty or even thirty feet above the level of the streets on which Jesus walked. Pointing out a par-

The Western (Wailing) Wall in Jerusalem early on Pentecost morning, when thousands of Jews have come for prayers. 5.2

73

ticular building as the site of the upper room in which Jesus and the disciples ate the Last Supper is obviously a relatively recent tradition. The burial site for King David on Mount Zion is likewise questionable. Two tombs recently excavated on Mount Ophel within the ancient city of David are much more likely to be the burial sites of David and Solomon. In spite of the false claims and late traditions, it is a moving experience to visit the city that has a biblical history all the way from Melchizedek and Abraham down to Christ and the beginning of the church.

The Wailing Wall
Harold Hazelip

Background Reading: *Luke 2:21–38; Mark 11:7–14; Acts 2:42–47; Acts 5:17–23*

The Wailing Wall, also known as the Western Wall, is a section of the wall which surrounded the Herodian temple and formed the support of the high platform of the temple complex. The height of the wall is some seventy feet with some sixteen more courses of stone under the current ground level. The wall is exposed for some 165 feet, only a small part of the total 1,560-foot Western Wall.

The Jews write down their wishes and prayers on small bits of paper, fold them carefully, and insert them into crevices between the stones of the Wailing Wall. They believe the messages will be read by God. The practice is several centuries old.

When David had finished his house and had defeated his enemies, he said to Nathan the prophet, "See now, I dwell in a house of cedar, but the ark of God dwells in a tent" (2 Sam. 7:2). Nathan told him to build a temple, but that night God told Nathan that David's son would be the one to build the house for God. God said, "You

[David] have shed much blood and have waged great wars; you shall not build a house to my name" (1 Chron. 22:8). Nathan relayed God's message and David yielded (2 Sam. 7). David collected materials for the future temple, including one hundred thousand talents of gold and one million talents of silver. David provided bronze, iron, wood, jewels, and stones. He also had craftsmen trained to carry out the work (1 Chron. 22, 28, and 29).

Solomon's Temple

Solomon was given instructions for the building of the temple and charged to carry out what David had planned for. David charged the leaders to help Solomon. He also spelled out arrangements for the temple services, for the duties of the priests, the music, the gatekeepers, the treasuries, officers, and judges (1 Chron. 22–27).

Construction began in April/May 966 B.C. and was completed in October/November 959 B.C. The laborers were Israelite men but Hiram and the Phoenicians furnished both the lumber and the skilled craftsmen (1 Kings 5). The logs were floated from Tyre to Joppa and then brought over land to Jerusalem (2 Chron. 2:16).

The basic plan for the temple approximately doubled the dimensions of the tabernacle, but retained the general layout of courtyard, porch, and double chamber. The building was ninety feet long, thirty feet wide, and forty-five feet high (1 Kings 6:2). When the temple was built, the stone was prepared at the quarry so that no hammers or axes broke the silence of the site. The Holy of Holies was a cube lined with paneling, separated from the Holy Place by a partition of cedar paneling, with double doors of olive wood (1 Kings 6:16, 20, 31, 32).

Solomon dedicated the temple by bringing the ark

into the Holy of Holies, making a speech, praying a long prayer, blessing the people, and offering up sacrifice on the new altar (1 Kings 8). The dedication apparently took eight days.

When the prayer had been completed and Solomon's sacrifices consumed, the glory of the Lord filled the temple (2 Chron. 7:1). The temple became the dwelling place of God and typified the way of salvation by which man can come into the presence of God (Heb. 8:1–15; 9:23, 24).

As the result of widespread apostasy characterized by the building of high places, in Rehoboam's fifth year Shishak was permitted to attack and take the treasures of the temple as a measure of divine judgment (2 Chron. 12:2–9). Asa put the votive gifts of his father in the temple; and later when Baasha, king of Israel, made war on Judah, Asa used the silver and gold from the temple to buy an alliance with Ben-hadad of Damascus (1 Kings 15:15–24).

When Athaliah usurped the throne of Judah from Joash, the young boy was hidden in the temple until he was old enough to rule (2 Chron. 22:10—23:15). During the reign of Athaliah, the temple fell into disrepair, largely as a result of priestly carelessness. This continued until Joash decided to restore the temple. Since no money was available for repairs, either from the temple treasury or the king's budget, a box was set up for free-will offerings. As money was collected, the workmen were hired and repairs were made (2 Chron. 24:4–14).

The idolatry practiced by Athaliah was so influential that the people persuaded Joash to leave God when Jehoiada the priest died. Zechariah rebuked Joash and was stoned to death in the temple court. Shortly afterward an attack by Syria dealt Jerusalem a damaging blow and Joash sent the temple treasures to Hazael, king of Syria, as tribute (2 Chron. 24:15–24; cf. 2 Kings 12:17, 18).

Nebuchadnezzar carried Jehoiakim and the vessels of the temple into Babylonian captivity (2 Chron. 36:7). Additional vessels were taken out of the temple of Babylon during the reign of the succeeding king Jehoiachin. When Zedekiah rebelled against Nebuchadnezzar, the city fell and the temple with it. The vessels of precious metal were removed and the temple was burned. It seems that the ark, cherubim, and other wooden objects, now stripped of their gold, perished in the flames.

In the fourteenth year after the destruction of Jerusalem (572 B.C.), Ezekiel was taken back to Jerusalem in a vision. An angel measured the temple as he watched. The return of the Lord to the temple is pictured, and instructions about the altar are given (Ezek. 40–43).

The Second Temple

Cyrus ordered the temple of Jerusalem rebuilt (2 Chron. 36:22, 23). Soon after the return of the Jews, the altar was rebuilt and sacrifices were resumed (Ezra 3:1–7). In the second year after their return, they began to rebuild the structure. The completed foundation caused some to rejoice, but elderly people who had seen the temple of Solomon wept over the inferiority of the new one (Ezra 3:8–13). Opposition forced construction to halt but the prophets Haggai and Zechariah promoted the project and work began again (Ezra 5:1, 2). The temple was finally dedicated and the feast days were celebrated (Ezra 6:16–22).

Nothing in the Bible indicates that God's presence ever filled this second temple. It lasted until about 20 B.C. (a hundred years longer than Solomon's temple). when Herod remodeled it.

Herod's Temple

The New Testament has over one hundred references to the temple. Parts of the temple specifically mentioned in the New Testament include the pinnacle (Matt. 4:5), its noble stones (Luke 21:5), Solomon's portico (John 10:23; Acts 3:11; 5:12) and the Beautiful Gate (Acts 3:2, 10).

Shortly after his birth, Jesus was brought to the temple to be presented to the Lord. This involved a sacrifice of either two turtledoves or a pair of young pigeons by his parents (Luke 2:22–24). During this activity, a righteous man named Simeon sang praises to God while holding the baby in his arms (Luke 2:25–35). A prophetess named Anna who lived in the temple also came to adore Jesus (Luke 2:36–38).

The next recorded visit of Jesus to the temple was at age twelve when he stayed behind after the Passover and sat among the teachers, listening to them and asking them question (Luke 2:41–52). During his temptation by Satan he was brought to the pinnacle of the temple and urged to jump off in order to test God (Matt. 4:5–7). John's Gospel records several trips Jesus made to Jerusalem during his ministry. On the first trip, he cleansed the temple of the merchants selling animals and exchanging money.

Near the end of his life, Jesus' triumphal entry into Jerusalem climaxed when he went "into the temple; and when he had looked round at everything, as it was already late, he went out to Bethany with the twelve" (Mark 11:11). The next day he again cleansed the temple of those exchanging money and selling birds and animals. Hearing Jesus was in the temple, the lame and blind went to him and were healed (Matt. 21:14). "And he was teaching daily in the temple" (Luke 19:47).

Jesus engaged in controversy with the Pharisees in the temple area, and spoke warnings and woes to them

(Matt. 22–23). He sat down next to the treasury, observed the worshipers giving their money, and made a comment about a widow and her mites (Mark 12:41–44). Once, as they were leaving the temple, some of his disciples mentioned the buildings. He replied, "Truly, I say to you, there will not be left here one stone upon another, that will not be thrown down" (Matt. 24:2). As Jesus left the temple for the last time (the Gospels do not mention his going back), he predicted its destruction.

After Jesus' ascension, the disciples frequented the temple daily (Luke 24:53; Acts 2:46). Peter and John were on their way to pray in the temple when they met the lame man at the Beautiful Gate and healed him (Acts 3:1–10). Peter then addressed the people from Solomon's portico (Acts 3:11–26). After Peter and John were arrested and set free, and the disciples began sharing their possessions with others, Luke records, "Now many signs and wonders were done among the people by the hands of the apostles. And they were all together in Solomon's portico. None of the rest dared join them, but the people held them in high honor" (Acts 5:12, 13).

Shortly afterward, the apostles were arrested. Upon their release by an angel, they entered the temple at daybreak and taught (Acts 5:19–21). They were brought before the council but were released on the advice of Gamaliel. "And every day in the temple and at home they did not cease teaching and preaching Jesus as the Christ" (Acts 5:42).

When Paul took four men to the temple in connection with a vow they had made, the Jews were stirred up against him and seized him. Paul was dragged out of the temple, the gates were shut behind, and the mob would have killed him had not the Roman officials come to the rescue. He spoke to the crowd; when they refused to listen any longer, he was taken back to the barracks, where it became known that he was a Roman citizen (Acts 21:17—22:29).

Some call Herod's temple the "second temple," following the tradition that Herod merely remodeled the structure Zerubbabel had erected. Others insist on calling Herod's temple the "third temple," suggesting that he completely reworked the area. Construction of Herod's temple began about 20 B.C., with the basic structure taking about one-and-one-half years to complete, although subsidiary work was still being carried on nearly fifty years later (John 2:20).

According to Josephus, Titus attacked Jerusalem in August of A.D. 70. After the fall of most of the city, the temple area remained the last Jewish stronghold. In the attack on the sanctuary itself, the structure was accidentally set on fire, against the wish of Titus. The last of the temple complex, along with about six thousand people who sought refuge there, perished.

Eusebius (fourth century A.D.) mentioned that it was sad to see the temple area in destruction. He commented that the destruction had already lasted more than four times as long as the seventy years of ruin during the Babylonian captivity. The platform seems to have remained in ruins until the arrival of the Muslims in the mid-seventh century.

Dome of the Rock

Today the Dome of the Rock and the al-Aksa Mosque dominate the platform. The Dome of the Rock was erected in the mid-seventh century by Abd al-Malik. It is basically an octagonal structure, supporting a drum and dome. On each of the eight walls are five windows, while another twelve windows grace the drum. It is the oldest existing monument of Muslim architecture. Many repairs have been made to the building, the most recent being in the 1950s.

Each of the eight sides measures sixty-three feet,

and the mosque has a total diameter of 180 feet. The total height, not counting the crescent, is 108 feet. Four gates permit entrance to the structure.

Inside is the rock, some fifty-eight feet long, fifty-one feet across, and four to six-and-a-half feet high. Traditions place the offering of Isaac on Moriah, the threshing floor of Ornan, and the altar or Holy of Holies of the three Jewish temples on this rock. A Muslim legend claims that Mohammed ascended into the heavens astride his horse from this rock.

Jewish people assemble at the Western Wall to pray and lament, especially on the eve of the Sabbath and of festivals. The wall has symbolized Jerusalem for many generations, calling to their minds the ideal of Jewish independence and Jewish consciousness.

Pool of Siloam in Jerusalem where Jesus healed the blind man (John 9). 5.3

81

The Pool of Siloam

Batsell Barrett Baxter

Background Reading: *2 Samuel 5:6–9; 2 Chronicles 32:1–8; 2 Kings 20:20; John 9:1–7*

The Siloam Pool lies in the lower section of the ancient area of Jerusalem known as Ophel. Ophel is the southeastern hill which lies south of Mount Moriah (the temple mount), west of the Kidron Valley, and east of the Tyropoeon Valley. Jerusalem was first settled on Ophel, an area of about eleven acres, because water was readily available and also perhaps because the steep walls to the east and west made the height easy to defend.

The word *Siloam* means "sending" or "sender." The Arabic spelling is *Silwan*. This is the name of the modern Arab village in the Kidron Valley surrounding the Pool of Siloam and the Gihon Spring. It appears that the name of the old pool, which was built before Hezekiah and called "Sent," was transferred to the new pool, which was built by Hezekiah.

The Jebusite Shaft

When David was thirty-seven, he was anointed king over all Israel. At that point, he moved his capital from Hebron to Jerusalem. However, Jerusalem was in the hands of the Jebusites, who first had to be conquered. David told his leading military men, "Whoever would smite the Jebusites, let him get up the water shaft to attack the lame and the blind, who are hated by David's soul" (2 Sam. 5:8); furthermore he offered the position of commander of his army to the man who accomplished the task (1 Chron. 11:6). The Jebusites had constructed a horizontal tunnel from the Gihon Spring to the west. After digging ninety feet under the city, they hit a natural cave. From the cave they dug a vertical shaft forty-five feet long. From the top of the shaft, they fashioned a sloping curving tunnel some 135 feet long which ended in a staircase which led to the city's summit. During a siege, water could be gained by going down the stairs and sloping tunnel to the vertical shaft, which would act like a well.

Apparently it was this shaft to which David referred and which Joab climbed, gaining access to the city. Kathleen Kenyon wrote, "There is every reason to suppose that this watershaft is the method by which the Jebusites had access to the spring in time of war, and that it was the means whereby the capture of the town by David was achieved."

Hezekiah's Tunnel

At a later time, when Hezekiah was king of Israel, the Assyrian king Sennacherib invaded Palestine and ultimately besieged Jerusalem. In anticipation of his approach Hezekiah made elaborate preparations. "He planned with his officers and his mighty men to stop the water of the springs that were outside the city; and they helped him. A great many people were gathered, and they stopped all the springs and the brook that flowed through the land, saying, 'Why should the kings of Assyria come and find much water?'" (2 Chron. 32:3, 4). Then, he had a tunnel dug to channel the water inside the city to what became known as the Pool of Siloam.

An S-shaped underground tunnel was discovered in 1867 by Charles Warren; it wound through the rock underneath Mount Ophel some 1,749 feet to the Pool of Siloam. The Gihon and Siloam Pool are only about 900 feet apart but the tunnel winds to make up the extra distance. The tunneling was done by starting at both ends and, by a remarkable feat of engineering, finally meeting in the middle. Hezekiah's engineers planned so expertly that when workmen, beginning at opposite ends of the tunnel, met, they were off only about twelve inches in elevation.

When Sennacherib laid siege to Jerusalem he and his men were unable to use the water which Hezekiah had brought within the city. Ultimately God miraculously destroyed 185,000 Assyrian soldiers and the remainder of the force was withdrawn (2 Kings 19:35, 36). In summarizing Hezekiah's reign, 2 Kings 20:20 says, "The rest of the deeds of Hezekiah, and all his might, and how he made the pool and the conduit and brought water into the city, are they not written in the Book of the Chronicles of the Kings of Judah?"

It is possible for visitors to Jerusalem today to walk through Hezekiah's tunnel. For us, it proved to be one of the most rewarding experiences of our trip. The passageway is two to three feet wide and five to six feet high and there is a constant stream of water passing through it. Normally the water is only a foot or so deep, so wading is easy, but occasionally the Gihon Spring gushes forth in an abundance of water and the tunnel may be filled nearly to the top. The spring gushes forth intermittently from a natural cave one or two times a day, though in the rainy season, it may issue forth four or five times a day. The water is cool and clear and fills the Siloam Pool at the southern end of the tunnel with beautiful, clear water. Eighteen stone steps descend to the present Pool of Siloam, which is fifty by fifteen feet. Stumps of ancient columns can still be seen in the water.

The Man Born Blind

While in Jerusalem for the feast of the Tabernacles (John 7:2) Jesus and his disciples passed a man who was born blind. The disciples used him as the basis for a question, "Rabbi, who sinned, this man or his parents, that he was born blind?" (John 9:2). Jesus replied that sin had not brought about his blindness—the man was born blind so that the power of God could be demonstrated. Jesus made some clay by spitting on the ground and spread it on the man's eyes. He told the man to go and wash in the Pool of Siloam. The man went, washed, and returned, seeing.

At another time those who were talking with Jesus told him of several Galileans who, while sacrificing, were attacked and killed by Pilate's soldiers. Jesus asked, "Do you think that these Galileans were worse sinners than all the other Galileans, because they suffered thus?" He responded that there was no connection between their suffering and sin and that all needed to repent. He then used the illustration of the eighteen people who were killed when the Tower of Siloam fell (Luke 13:1–4).

In a city where traditions reign and false claims are constantly being made, the visitor finds it refreshing to locate something that by its very nature has to be authentic. The tunnel of Hezekiah is a good example. Such a tunnel through solid rock beneath the city could not be moved nor its course changed. The pool at the end of the tunnel may differ in size or in appearance, but it must be at the same location as the pool known in Jesus' day. It was here, at this exact location, that a man washed the clay from his eyes and could see. Walking in this tunnel and wading in the Pool of Siloam provided a memorable experience.

REVIEW

1. In what ways is Jerusalem a divided city today?
2. Why has the Golden Gate worn three names?
3. How is it possible for us to get an idea of how Jerusalem looked in Jesus' day?
4. What was Jerusalem like in the days of Christ?
5. Describe modern Jerusalem.
6. What is the biblical significance of the Pool of Siloam?

Describe the Pool of Siloam today.

7. What is the Wailing Wall actually? How did the "Wailing Wall" get its name? What is the significance of the Wailing Wall to the Jews?

CHAPTER SIX

Jerusalem—the Holy City

The Garden of Gethsemane with the Golden Gate in the distance.   6.1

The Garden of Gethsemane

Batsell Barrett Baxter

Background Reading: *Luke 21:37, 38; Matthew 26:36–50*

The Garden of Gethsemane is located at the foot of the western slope of the Mount of Olives in the Kidron Valley. The name *Gethsemane*, found in Matthew 26:36 and Mark 14:32, means "oil press." The name of the site probably came from an olive oil press located on the hillside at some point in history. It is altogether

0   500   1000   2000
Scale of Feet

Jerusalem

natural that such a press would be located on a mountain that abounded in olive trees, as suggested by the name *Mount of Olives*.

The Kidron Valley, which is only three miles long, separates Jerusalem on the west and the Mount of Olives on the east. The actual bed of the valley today is thought to be some ten to fifty feet above the level of the valley in ancient times due to the accumulation of debris over the centuries. Two springs provide the valley with water, the Gihon and the En-rogel.

The Davidic kings owned property in the Kidron Valley; this led to its being called the King's Valley. David crossed the valley when he fled from Absalom (2 Sam. 15:23). Absalom set up a monument for himself in the King's Valley (2 Sam. 18:18).

In Jeremiah 31:40 the prophet looked forward to the day when the city would be rebuilt and even the places of burial would be sacred to God. The verse reads, "The whole valley of the dead bodies and the ashes, and all the fields as far as the brook Kidron, to the corner of the Horse Gate toward the east, shall be sacred to the Lord. It shall not be uprooted or overthrown any more for ever." G. A. Barrois wrote that this passage "opened the way for all sorts of symbolic interpretations." Key among these was the interpretation of Kidron as the Valley of Jehoshaphat. This identification results from such passages as Joel 3:1, 2 which states, "In those days. . . . I will gather all the nations and bring them down to the valley of Jehoshaphat, and I will enter into judgment with them there, on account of my people and my heritage Israel, because they have scattered them among the nations, and have divided up my land." Verse 12 reads, "Let the nations bestir themselves, and come up to the valley of Jehoshaphat; for there I will sit to judge all the nations round about." The tradition arising from this interpretation can be traced back to the fourth century A.D. It has led many to believe that the final judgment will take place at this site. It is for this reason that many have wished to be buried in the area, thinking that there will be some special advantage on the great judgment day.

A Garden of Prayer

Our interest in this area is based on evidence far more solid than these traditions. The Scriptures plainly declare that on the night of Christ's betrayal Jesus and the faithful apostles left the upper room and went out to the Mount of Olives (Matt. 26:30; Mark 14:26), as was his custom (Luke 22:39). The site was located just across the Kidron Valley (John 18:1) where there was a garden known by the name *Gethsemane.* The Synoptic Gospels give the impression that the area was large enough for the apostles and Jesus to be a good distance from one another. Leaving the group, Jesus took Peter, James, and John with him a bit further into the garden; then he left them and went still further to pray alone. It was here that he prayed, "Father, if thou art willing, remove this cup from me; nevertheless not my will, but thine, be done" (Luke 22:42; cf. Matt. 26:39; Mark 14:35). Luke records that his agony was so intense that his sweat was like great drops of blood. When he came back to his apostles, he found them sleeping. He left them a second and a third time, praying earnestly that the cup of suffering might pass from him; each time when he returned he found them asleep (Matt. 26:42–46). Soon Judas came leading a multitude, carrying swords, clubs, and lanterns, and guided the officials to Jesus, whom he identified with a kiss. Jesus readily admitted his identity, was arrested, and led away to be subjected to a series of hastily arranged, illegal trials. His followers left him and fled (Matt. 26:47–56).

The Crucial Decision

It was in the Garden of Gethsemane that the Son of God made the final decision which made possible the eternal salvation of the entire human race. It is awesome to contemplate the magnitude of this decision: "My Father, if this cannot pass unless I drink it, thy will be done" (Matt. 26:42). The quiet beauty of the garden today, amid the centuries-old olive trees, belies the titanic struggle which took place there nearly two thousand years ago. Even then, outwardly, it was a pleasant, restful place where Jesus frequently retreated for prayer and for private sessions with his apostles (Luke 21:37; John 18:2).

The Bible does not give enough information to pinpoint the exact location of the garden where Jesus prayed. Only that it was on the west side of the Mount of Olives seems clear. Today the uncertainty is illustrated by the fact that four different sites are revered by leading religious groups: the Russians, the Armenians, the Greek Orthodox, and the Roman Catholics.

Josephus indicates that the area east of Jerusalem was cleared by the Romans, who "cut down all the trees there were in the country that adjoined to the city, and that for ninety furlongs round about" when they besieged Jerusalem during the first century A.D. at the time of the Jewish revolt. If this is true, the present-day ancient gnarled olive trees, while quite old, do not go back to the time of Jesus.

The Christian who visits the western slope of the Mount of Olives today finds the rival claims concerning the exact site of the Garden of Gethsemane somewhat disquieting. The commercialism that has grown up with the tourist trade and the elaborate, ornate church buildings and memorials which have been erected seem out of place. He finds himself wishing for a period of uninterrupted quiet in which to meditate upon the fact that somewhere on this hillside the spiritual des-

The Garden Tomb in Jerusalem. 6.2

91

tiny of the human race hung in the balance as Jesus prayed and then submitted his will to the will of God.

Christ's Tomb

Batsell Barrett Baxter

Background Reading: *John 19:17-30; John 19:31-42; John 20:1-10*

Jesus was led from the palace, the place of the pavement, to be crucified. On the way his captors made Simon of Cyrene carry his cross. A great crowd followed Jesus on his death path, including a large number of crying women. Jesus told them not to cry for him, but for themselves. Two other men were also to be crucified.

They arrived at Golgotha, an Armaic word meaning "the skull." The word appears only three times in the Bible (Matt. 27:33; Mark 15:22; John 19:17). Golgotha was located near Jerusalem. Hebrews 13:12 indicates that Jesus suffered outside the city walls. However, the site was not far outside the walls, but "near the city" (John 19:20). Matthew's statement, "And those who passed by . . ." (Matt. 27:39), may indicate that Golgotha was by a well-traveled road. It was visible from some distance, as indicated by the expression, "women looking on from afar" (Mark 15:40; cf. Luke 23:49). This has led some to think it was a hill, but nowhere does the Bible indicate that the crucifixion took place on a hill. Further, only in John 19:41 is there indication that the tomb was near the site of death and that it was in a garden. All of these suggestions do not enable us to locate the site of the crucifixion and burial with absolute certainty.

Upon his arrival at Golgotha, wherever it was, the officers gave Jesus a drink of wine mixed with gall, but he refused it. Jesus was crucified with two thieves, and while dying uttered seven meaningful sayings, among which are: "My God, my God, why have you forsaken me?" "Father, into your hands I commend my spirit," and "It is finished." When he died the earth quaked, tombs were opened, and darkness came upon the earth at midday. The Roman centurion in charge of the crucifixion said, "Truly this was the Son of God." Having found Jesus dead within a relatively short time, the Roman soldiers pierced his side (Matt. 27:32–56; Mark 15:21–41; Luke 23:26–49; John 19:17–37).

The Holy Sepulcher

From early times Christians have regarded the site of the Church of the Holy Sepulcher as the place of Christ's death, burial, and resurrection. Tradition states that the site of Calvary was taken by the Romans, where they erected a statue of Jupiter-Serapis, while over the tomb they constructed an altar to Venus. In A.D. 326 Constantine exposed the tomb and began to build a basilica. The tomb was covered before the end of that century by a rotunda thirty-seven feet high and forty feet in diameter. The church was destroyed in 614 A.D. by the Persians but immediately it was rebuilt. A separate church was built over the site of Calvary; it was not until the tenth century that the two sites were brought into one building as they are today. The current Church of the Holy Sepulcher was constructed by the Crusaders.

The Garden Tomb

There are many today who believe that the Garden Tomb, rather than the Church of the Holy Sepulcher, is the true site of Christ's burial. This controversy is not new. Some sixteen theories concerning the site of the death and burial of Jesus were promoted between 1840 and 1876, of which twelve argued in favor of the Holy

Sepulcher and the other four against it. In 1840, Otto Thenius first suggested that the hillock outside the Damascus Gate, with ancient cisterns dug into its side, was the authentic Calvary.

In 1882 General Charles (Chinese) Gordon, while sitting on the roof of a house in Jerusalem, noted that the hill behind the present-day Arab bus station looked just like a skull. Two small dark caves formed the eyes, a ridge made the nose, and a lower opening in the ragged cliff suggested the mouth. It gave the clear impression of a skull. In 1867, a Greek doing construction work at the foot of the hill had found a rock-hewn tomb there. The tomb was cut from solid rock and was assigned by some to Roman times, but by others to the Byzantine period.

No tradition earlier than the nineteenth century regards the site of Gordon's Calvary or the Garden Tomb as authentic. The site of the Garden Tomb is 650 feet north of the present Damascus Gate, a part of the modern wall of Jerusalem. The tomb is cut into solid rock and is fourteen feet wide, ten feet deep, and seven-and-one-half feet high. The controversy as to whether the Church of the Holy Sepulcher or the Garden Tomb is the site of Christ's death and burial continues to rage. It is noteworthy that both sites are merely the suggestions of tradition.

Archaeologists and historians of first-century A.D. Jerusalem speak of three walls of the city. The current walls were built in fairly recent times and are thought to follow the walls built by Hadrian in the second century. Therefore, the question is not where the walls fall today, but where they stood in the first century. The authenticity of the Holy Sepulcher site depends in part upon where the second wall of the city rested. If it curved to the west, the Holy Sepulcher would have been inside the city and thus would be removed as a possible site of the death of Jesus. However, if it curved to the east then the church remains a possible site. At present it is impossible to establish the course of the second wall and to determine with certainty whether the Church of the Holy Sepulcher was in or outside of Herod's city of Jerusalem at the time when Jesus was crucified.

As a postscript to the above uncertainties, let us remember that it is not exactly where, or even when, Christ was crucified, buried, and raised from the dead that matters, but the fact that it happened. Actually, it matters little whether the site of the Holy Sepulcher or the site of the Garden Tomb is the correct one. The point of supreme importance is that Jesus lived, died, and lives again. This is a part of the solid evidence that he is the divine Son of God and our Savior.

A religious procession follows the traditional *via dolorosa* or "way of sorrows" through old Jerusalem. 6.3

The Via Dolorosa

Harold Hazelip

Background Reading: *Luke 23:26–33; Matthew 27:27–37*

The Via Dolorosa, or "Way of Sorrows," is the traditional path followed by Jesus from his condemnation by Pilate until his death on the cross. The present ground level is many feet above what it was in the first century. Accordingly, the sites we see today do not date back to the time of Jesus. Excavation, however, has uncovered some first-century remains.

From Gethsemane to Calvary

After his arrest Jesus had been taken first to the house of Annas, the father-in-law of the high priest Caiaphas. Before Annas, Jesus was asked about his disciples and his teaching. When he answered, Jesus was struck by one of the soldiers standing near. Annas sent him bound to Caiaphas (John 18:12–27).

Jesus was then tried before Caiaphas, the high priest, and before the scribes and elders that were gathered. To accuse him they hired false witnesses, but unfortunately for them, the testimony of the witnesses was contradictory. Unable to make their case with false witnesses, they began to question Jesus. His replies threw them into a frenzy. They decided he had blasphemed and was worthy of death. They spat in his face and beat him with the palms of their hands. They hit him and then asked him to identify the person who had done the striking (Matt. 26:57–68).

The next morning Jesus' accusers took him to Pilate the governor. They did not want to enter the hall because they would defile themselves for the Passover. Pilate came out to them and exchanged remarks concerning Jesus; finally, he told them to try Jesus themselves. They replied that he deserved death and this required Roman approval. At this point, Jesus was asked by Pilate if he were the king of the Jews. During the ensuing conversation Pilate asked his famous question, "What is truth?" After the examination, Pilate told the Jews outside he could find no reason to condemn the man (John 18:28–38).

When Pilate learned that Jesus was from the northern part of Palestine, he sent him to Herod, who happened to be visiting in Jerusalem. Herod was glad to see him because Jesus had acquired a reputation and Herod wanted to see a miracle. Herod also had a number of questions for Jesus, which Jesus refused to answer. All during the trial the Jews kept up a steady stream of accusations. Soldiers mocked Jesus, dressing him in royal robes (Luke 23:6–12).

Jesus was sent back to Pilate, who announced that he had decided Jesus was innocent and that Herod agreed. He indicated that Jesus would be chastised and then released (Luke 23:13–16). Since the governor usually released one prisoner at Passover, Pilate offered the people a choice between the notorious Barabbas and Jesus. He knew the accusations were brought against Jesus because of the envy of the Jewish leaders (Matt. 27:15–18).

About this time, Pilate's wife sent a message that she had had a bad dream about Jesus and warned Pilate against harming him. Jewish officials stirred up the crowd, and when Pilate made his offer, the people asked for Barabbas. When Pilate asked what to do with Jesus, the crowd ordered him to be crucified (Matt. 27:19–23). Pilate made his appeal three times, but the crowds were insistent that Jesus should be killed (Luke 23:22–24).

Pilate saw that a riot was developing, so he took a bowl of water and symbolically washed his hands of the affair in full view of the crowds. Pilate then had Jesus scourged and taken into the palace. The soldiers on duty stripped him and put on him a scarlet robe and a crown made of thorns. They placed a reed in his right hand, mockingly bowed in front of him, spat on him, and hit him with the reed (Matt. 27:24–31).

Pilate went back out to the crowd and indicated that he had found nothing wrong in Jesus. The soldiers brought Jesus out and Pilate presented him: "Behold the man!" During Pilate's conversation with the crowd, he became aware of the fact that Jesus was claiming to be the Son of God. This worried Pilate and he went back into the palace to talk more with Jesus. The more they talked the more Pilate wanted to release him. But when he confronted the Jews with his renewed intentions to release Jesus, they accused Pilate of not being loyal to Caesar. He brought Jesus to the Pavement called *Gabbatha* in Hebrew, and decided to crucify him (John 19:4–16).

"Stations of the Cross"

At this point in the narrative tradition has entered to establish fourteen stops or stations between Pilate's palace and Golgotha. These stations mark events reported in the Gospels or invented by tradition. Each Friday at three o'clock in the afternoon the Franciscans retrace the steps of the tradition.

Station One marks the site where Jesus was condemned. The building today is a Muslim school called El-Omariye. Entrance is gained by a flight of steps. Tradition holds that this was the site of the Praetorium, where Pilate's judgment hall was located and Jesus was sentenced. The original staircase, known as the Scala Santa, is supposed to have been taken to Rome by Helena. Today it is displayed in the church near St. Giovanni in Laterano.

Station Two marks the site where Jesus received the cross. The station is located on the road outside Station

One opposite the Chapel of the Condemnation. Under the arch Pilate said, "Behold the man." Nearby is a Greek Orthodox monastery which claims to be the site of the prison of Barabbas.

Station Three marks the spot where Jesus fell the first time. It is around the corner, positioned to the left of the second station, where there is a small museum and a store. This station does not mark a biblical event but a probable tradition.

Station Four marks the site where Jesus met his mother. The area is marked by an Armenian Catholic church built in 1881. Tradition says that Mary exchanged a glance with Jesus and that, when Jesus fell, she pushed through the crowd to comfort him.

Station Five marks the place where Simon the Cyrenian took the cross from Jesus (Luke 23:26). This station was constructed by the Franciscans in 1895.

Station Six marks the place where Veronica wiped the face of Jesus. Tradition states that she was one of the weeping women who followed Jesus. Tradition further states that Veronica was the lady who had an issue of blood for twelve years before Jesus healed her. The cloth, which allegedly contains the blood and sweat from Jesus' face and the imprint of his features, is in St. Peter's in Rome.

Station Seven marks the place where Jesus fell the second time. Across from the station is a column where some say the Romans fastened the death sentence. It is called the Gate of Judgment. The Franciscans bought the site of Station Seven in 1875.

Station Eight recalls where Jesus spoke to the daughters of Jerusalem (Luke 23:28). It is marked by a stone with a Latin cross and the Greek word *nikē* (victory).

Station Nine marks the place where Jesus allegedly fell a third time. The station, located up a flight of twenty-eight steps, is marked by the shaft of a column enclosed in a pillar of the door of a Coptic church.

Station Ten marks the place where Jesus was stripped of his clothes. Stations Ten through Thirteen are at the traditional site of Calvary.

Station Eleven marks the site where Jesus was nailed to the cross. It is located in the right nave of the Church of the Holy Sepulcher, the section which belongs to the Franciscans. The site is marked by a silver-covered altar made in Florence in 1558 and by a mosaic made in 1938.

Station Twelve marks the place where Jesus died on the cross. A disc marks the spot where the cross was fixed. On a platform two feet high stands a Greek altar.

Station Thirteen recalls the taking down of the body of Jesus from the cross. Over the altar is a wood statue from the sixteenth century.

Station Fourteen is the tomb in the Church of the Holy Sepulcher.

The Church of the Holy Sepulcher

Six religious communities have certain rights in the Church of the Holy Sepulcher today. These rights are protected by the "Status Quo," an arrangement dating from 1757 which states that there will be no change or innovation either in possession or in the exercise of ritual. The six groups are the Franciscans, Greek Orthodox, Armenian Orthodox, Syrian, Coptic, and Abyssinian. The Copts have two rooms, and a chapel at the rear of the sepulcher itself, but are restricted to certain days. The Syrians and Abyssinians are even more limited in their rights. These rights include the use of lamps, decorations, pictures, and candles, as well as the rights to clean and make repairs. These rights are worked out in detail since the right to repair a wall or to hang a picture implies possession of that wall or picture.

There is a paved court in front of the Church of the

Holy Sepulcher. It measures some fifty-four by eighty feet, and lies over an ancient cistern. A number of chapels mark each side. The court was the scene of bloodshed on a number of occasions when various religious communities came to blows over the rights of the sanctuary. The last such occasion was in November, 1901, when fifteen Franciscans were wounded by Greek monks.

The door on the right has been closed since the time of the Crusades, while the key and the right to open the other door are in the hands of two Muslim families. Entrance is free, the fee being paid by the community using the basilica. Once inside, the Muslim doorkeepers rest on the left. Some say they are there to keep the rival Christian groups at peace with one another.

Directly in front of the door (on the inside) is a polished red stone measuring about four by eight feet. It is called the "Stone of Anointing"; it marks the place where Joseph and Nicodemus prepared the body of Jesus for burial. On the right is Calvary, which is some seventeen feet above the floor of the building and measures thirty by thirty-seven feet. The top is divided into two chapels; the one on the right belongs to the Latins. About one-third of the platform rests on the rock below, the remainder rests on structure. A silver disc with an opening in the center marks the spot where the cross was fixed. On each side of the altar is a black marble disc marking the hole where the cross of one of the thieves stood. On the right of the altar is the place where the rock was split by the earthquake. The crack runs through the entire rock and can be seen below in the Chapel of Adam.

Under the dome is the *Anastasis* or the site of the sepulcher itself. The upper narrow gallery belongs to the Greeks; the lower, wider gallery is divided between the Latins and the Armenians. In the center is the sepulcher—twenty-seven feet long, nineteen feet wide and high, covered with marble and adorned with sixteen pillars.

Scattered throughout the building are numerous other sites marking biblical and postbiblical events. Included are the spots where the women watched the crucifixion, the place from which the Jewish officials mocked Jesus, the place where the soldiers divided his clothes, the place where Jesus appeared to Mary, and the column of the flagellation. It should be mentioned again that the many claims made are, of course, to be regarded as traditions rather than as proven facts.

REVIEW

1. What is the significance of the Dome of the Rock?
2. Why is the Golden Gate walled up?
3. What is the Garden of Gethsemane like today?
4. Is it possible to locate the actual tomb in which Jesus was laid? What is "Gordon's Tomb"?
5. How would you feel if you had been with the disciples on that day when the tomb was found empty? What would you have thought when you saw that rock rolled back?
6. What does "Via Dolorosa" mean? Where is it, and why was it named that?
7. What are the "Stations of the Cross"?
8. What happens in Jerusalem each Friday at 3 p.m.?
9. Describe the unusual manner in which The Church of the Holy Sepulcher is divided. Can we depend on it for historical accuracy?

CHAPTER SEVEN

You Will Be My Witnesses

Jesus ascended to his Father from the Mount
of Olives, just east of Jerusalem. 7.1

Mount of Olives
Batsell Barrett Baxter

Background Reading: *Luke 19:35–44; Matthew
24:3–14; Acts 1:9–12*

The mountain directly east of the city of Jerusalem
is known as the Mount of Olives, suggesting the abundance of olive trees upon its slopes in ancient times.
The mountain is called "Mount of the Ointment" in the
Talmud. It was a Sabbath-day's journey from the city,
meaning three thousand feet or five stadia.

The Mount of Olives is actually a ridge which runs

103

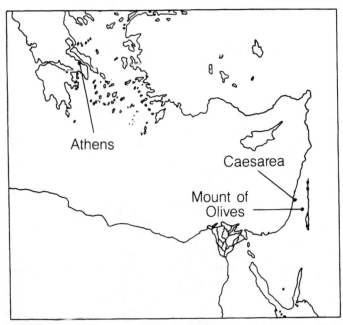

along the east side of the city of Jerusalem parallel to
the ravine known as the Kidron Valley. There are three
separate peaks on the ridge; these are known today as
Mount Scopus, the Mount of Olives, and the Mount of
Offense. The entire ridge is about two-and-one-half
miles long. The northernmost peak, at an altitude of
2,963 feet above sea level, is the highest. Its name,
Scopus, comes from a word which indicates seeing, or
overlooking, in this case, the city of Jerusalem. We also
get our modern terms *microscope* and *telescope* from
this word. The famous Hebrew University has been
erected on top of this mountain.

The middle peak rises about 100 feet higher than
Jerusalem at approximately 2,700 feet above sea level.
Looking to the east, one has a magnificent view of the
Jordan Valley and the Dead Sea (on a clear day) some
fourteen miles away and some 4,000 feet down in the
Great Rift. Beyond are the mountains of Moab, while
to the southeast is the area known as the wilderness of

Judea, the site of the temptations of Jesus. Looking west from the mountain, one has a beautiful panoramic view of the city of Jerusalem, with the temple mount and its Muslim holy buildings in the foreground and the Old and the New City behind. In addition to olive trees, there are abundant stands of pines near the top of the mountain. The wind blows quite hard in this area, bending the trees in a permanent southeastern direction. The Mount of Olives has a special meaning for us, because it was our home during our stay in Jerusalem. The Intercontinental Hotel, erected on the southern brow of the Mount of Olives, provides a magnificent view of Jerusalem, just across the Kidron Valley to the west.

The southernmost peak, which some do not even consider part of the same ridge, is called the Mount of Offense, the Mount of Corruption, the Mount of Evil Counsel, or Mount Scandal, because Solomon is thought to have built pagan altars here for his foreign wives (1 Kings 11:7, 8).

From the biblical narrative it appears that Bethany was on the east side of the Mount of Olives, with Bethphage located nearby, possibly a bit nearer to the top of the mountain. The Garden of Gethsemane was on the lower slope of the Mountain toward the west.

Biblical Events

A number of events during Christ's ministry occurred on or near the Mount of Olives. Apparently Jesus spent the final week of his life before the crucifixion teaching in Jerusalem during the daytime, but retiring to the Mount of Olives each evening. His triumphal entry crossed the mountain as he came from Bethany to Jerusalem at the beginning of the week. On his way into the city on one of the mornings he saw a fig tree and because of its barrenness caused it to wither away. According to Luke, it was from the Mount of Olives that Jesus looked down upon the city of Jerusalem and wept over it because of its sinful rebellion against God (Luke 19:41, 42). After having preached in the temple area, Jesus returned to the Mount of Olives and sat down with his disciples to answer their questions concerning the destruction of the temple and the end of the world (Matt. 24–25; Mark 13).

The Mount of Olives was also the site of the ascension of Jesus. Jesus had predicted his ascension, talking about "his departure" (Luke 9:31), and the fact that "the days drew near for him to be received up" (Luke 9:51). John indicated that he would be glorified (John 7:39; 12:16, 23). Mark indicated that Jesus "was taken up into heaven, and sat down at the right hand of God" (Mark 16:19).

According to Luke, Jesus taught his disciples about the fulfillment of Old Testament prophecy and about their role in proclaiming his death and resurrection. Then he led them as far as Bethany, where he lifted up his hands and blessed them. While Jesus was blessing his disciples he was carried away into heaven. The disciples returned to Jerusalem and were constantly in the temple (Luke 24:44–53). Acts also tells about the final conversation with the disciples and about the ascension, including the testimony of two angels that he would return in like manner (Acts 1:6–12).

Divergent Claims

There are three sites claimed for the ascension, two Jericho roads, three paths of the triumphal entry, and four Gardens of Gethsemane. These divergent claims are, to say the least, distracting. In spite of the fact that no one can know with absolute certainty the specific spots where the events in the life of Jesus occurred, many buildings have been built claiming identification with this or that event. When Constantine, the first

"Christian" emperor, built churches in Palestine, he built at three sites: the places of the birth, resurrection, and ascension of Jesus. The church which he started at the ascension site in A.D. 325 was destroyed in 614 by the Persians. The church was in part restored, according to the testimony of Arculf in 670, but it was pulled down again by al-Hakim in 1010. The Crusaders rebuilt on the ruins and other rebuildings have taken place in later centuries.

At a slightly different site Arculf saw a structure which had a series of concentric circles with doors leading into the innermost circle. The inner room was without a roof and in the center were, it was claimed, the last footprints of the Lord before he ascended. This structure was rebuilt by the Crusaders as an octogon and Saladin converted it into a mosque, adding a roof. The most impressive building today is the Russian

Roman theater at Caesarea was built by Herod the Great. 7.2

Orthodox Monastery belltower on the crest of the mountain. Built sometime in the nineteenth century, the tower has six stories and 214 steps.

On the slope of the Mount of Olives, facing the temple area, is the largest and oldest Jewish cemetery in the world. Dating back to biblical times, it is a choice burial site because many expect the resurrection to take place first on the Mount of Olives. Tradition holds that those buried here will be raised first. Reference to Zechariah 14:1–11 is made. For those of us who are not likely to be buried there, it is comforting to remember that when Jesus returns, the righteous of all the earth will be caught up to meet him in the clouds to be with him forever (1 Thess. 4:16–18).

Caesarea

Harold Hazelip

Background Reading: *Acts 10:1–8, 23–48; Acts 23:23–35*

Coastal Caesarea is to be distinguished from Caesarea Philippi. The city of Caesarea on the Mediterranean Sea is uninhabited today. It is located midway between Haifa and Tel Aviv, in the midst of the very fertile Plain of Sharon. This area is known today for its citrus fruit. The Mount Carmel range is about eight miles to the north.

Herod's City
According to Josephus, Herod the Great observed that "there was a city by the seaside that was much decayed, [but] was capable of improvements." This city was Strato's Tower. Herod "rebuilt it with white stone,

and adorned it with several most spendid palaces"
(25–13 B.C.). Herod had noted that there was no good
haven for ships from Dora to Joppa and that the sailors
were "obliged to lie in the stormy sea." Herod "over-
came nature and built a haven larger than Piraeus [the
port of Athens]." Josephus notes that "abutting the
harbor were houses, also of white stone, and upon it
converge the streets of the town, laid at equal distances
apart."

Herod renamed the city Caesarea after Augustus
Caesar (emperor of Rome from 27 B.C. to A.D. 14, who
had given Herod the title of king). Caesar's temple,
"remarkable for its beauty and grand proportions,"
stood facing the harbor. Josephus notes that the buildings in the city were "all constructed in a style worthy
of the name which the city bore." Herod also "appointed games every fifth year and called them in like
manner 'Caesar's Games.'"

The harbor is considered one of Herod's most remarkable building works. Three hundred yards south
of the harbor stand the remains of a Roman theater.
Excavated from 1959 to 1964, the theater was built by
Herod. Concerning the theater one writer commented,
"The rulers of those times were neither the most hu-
mane nor the most refined people in history but they
knew how to build. And they knew where. The theater
is a monument to their taste and skill."

Caesarea also boasted a Roman hippodrome. This
race course, built inside the Herodian city, measures
1,056 feet by 264 feet. A square granite pillar, thirty-
five feet long, lies in the center of the complex, which
was able to seat twenty thousand spectators. Near the
pillar are three conical blocks which were polished to
shine like mirrors. These reflected the sun into the
horses' eyes during the race—resulting in frightened
horses and a more exciting race.

Biblical History

After the conversion of the Ethiopian in Acts 8, Philip passed on to Azotus and other towns until he came to Caesarea (Acts 8:40). He apparently settled here. On Paul's return from his third missionary journey, he stayed in Philip's home. Philip, who was known as an evangelist, was the father of four unmarried daughters who were known for their prophesying (Acts 21:8, 9).

A Roman army officer named Cornelius was stationed at Caesarea. Through a vision Cornelius, himself a Gentile, was told to send to Joppa, some thirty miles to the south, to ask the apostle Peter to come to Caesarea (Acts 10:1–8). Peter and the messengers of Cornelius, along with some Christians from Joppa, arrived in Caesarea to find a crowd in Cornelius' house. After some teaching and discussion, Cornelius and some of his associates became Christians (Acts 10:23–48). Peter remained in Caesarea for a number of days (Acts 10:48). He later went to Jerusalem, where he told the apostles of the events in Caesarea (Acts 11:11–17).

Toward the end of Paul's second missionary journey, he left Ephesus and sailed to Caesarea. On that occasion he visited the church and went on to Antioch (Acts 18:22). After completing his third missionary tour, he was arrested in Jerusalem. The officials decided to transfer Paul to the prison in Caesarea. He was moved there at night by an armed escort. Paul rode a horse on the fifty-mile trip from Jerusalem in the hills to Caesarea on the plain. Paul was delivered to Felix, who placed him in Herod's praetorium under guard (Acts 23:23–35).

During his imprisonment in Caesarea, Paul made several appearances before civil authorities. The first appearance occurred five days after Paul's arrival. The Jewish high priest, Ananias, along with some elders and their spokesman Tertullus, came to plead their case against Paul before Felix.

Paul was kept in custody but was allowed some freedom and visits from friends. He was arraigned before Felix and his wife Drusilla (a Jewess) to speak about the Christian faith. After some discussion, he was sent away. Felix later talked with Paul several times, hoping Paul would offer him money for pardon. The matter ended two years later when Felix was replaced and left Paul in prison (Acts 24).

Porcius Festus was the next governor and he heard Paul soon after his arrival. The Jews came from Jerusalem to present their case. As an attempt to please the Jews, Festus asked Paul if he would stand trial in Jerusalem. Paul appealed to Caesar (Acts 25:1–12).

Standing on Mar's Hill in Athens, with the Acropolis in the distance.   7.3

Paul also told his story before Festus and King Agrippa, along with Agrippa's wife Bernice. Following this speech it was decided that Paul would be sent to Rome (Acts 25:23—26:32).

The remains of Herod's city are scattered throughout the area today. Much of the building material used by Herod was reused by the Byzantines and the Crusaders. It is interesting to note that until the excavations at Caesarea were conducted, nothing was known of the Roman procurator Pontius Pilate except the material in the Gospels and Josephus. In the excavation of the theater a stone was found which bears this inscription (as restored): *Tiberieum/Pontius Pilatus/Praefectus Iudaeae*—"Tiberius [the Roman emperor of the period]/Pontius Pilate/Prefect of Judea."

Athens
Bill Humble

Background Reading: *Acts 17:16–34*

One of the most dramatic events in New Testament history must have been when Paul came to Athens alone on his second missionary journey, was challenged by the Epicurean and Stoic philosophers at the Areopagus (Mar's Hill), and preached the great sermon about the unknown god (Acts 17).

The "golden age" in Athens' history had come 500 years before Paul visited the city. Its rise to greatness began in the sixth century B.C. The constitution of Solon was adopted in 594 B.C. and was intended to safeguard the rights of the people. Under Cleisthenes at the end of the century, true democracy was born in Athens. The wars between Persia and Greece (490–479 B.C.) brought Athens to greater prominence. Even though the city was destroyed, the Athenian fleet played a decisive role in Persia's defeat. After the war the Athenians returned and rebuilt their city, and it soon became a strong commercial and maritime city.

Just after the Persian Wars, Pericles, the most enlightened politician of antiquity, made his appearance. During his years of leadership (443–429 B.C.), Athens came to her economic, cultural and artistic golden age. In government Athens was a democracy, and her example has been the beacon for man's struggle for freedom in the modern world. Great public buildings and temples were erected and were decorated by artists like Pheidias and Iktinos. The great writers, Aeschylus, Sophocles and Euripides, produced the dramas that were staged in beautiful theaters across Greece. Somehow, it was the fulness of time for the flowering of classical Greek civilization. Perhaps never again in human history would so few people in so few years achieve so much in government, architecture and building, literature, and art.

Tragically, this golden age for Athens was followed quickly by the terrible Peloponnesian War (431–404 B.C.) that set Athens against Sparta and ended in the defeat of Athens. But the city was resilient, and art and science flourished after the war. Democracy, though fragile, was restored for a century, until Philip of Macedon conquered all of Greece. The Macedonian empire soon gave way to Rome, and Athens fell under the control of the Romans in 146 B.C. The Roman general Sulla beseiged Athens and then allowed his soldiers to loot the city in 86 B.C. Later, thanks to her former glory, Athens enjoyed the favor of Roman emperors who adorned the city with new public buildings. But stripped of her power and commerce, Athens went into swift decline.

Thus, when Paul arrived in Athens about 50 A.D. on his second missionary journey, the city was poor. The power and prosperity of earlier centuries were long gone. What remained were the great public buildings and temples that reflected Athens' past glory and a reputation for learning and culture that still attracted students and visitors from throughout the Roman world.

When Paul saw Athens, the acropolis dominated the city, just as it does today. The acropolis is a hill of rock that is flat on the summit and about 450 feet high. In the early days of Athenian history, it was surrounded by a strong wall and was the site of the king's palace. Later, it became the sanctuary of the city, and sacred buildings were erected on it. These early temples were destroyed in the Persian Wars, but in the golden age of Athens that followed the wars, the acropolis was adorned with the beautiful temples that still fill visitors with awe and wonder.

The largest and most impressive of these buildings was the Parthenon, which was built of white pentelic marble between 447 B.C. and 438 B.C. Dedicated to the goddess Athena, the Parthenon is 238 feet long and 111 feet wide, with 46 columns that are 34 feet high. The sculptured pediments at either end depicted Greek mythology with the birth of Athena on the east end and the struggle of Athena and Poseidon for control of Attica on the west. Architecturally, the Parthenon has been called one of the most perfectly proportioned buildings ever built. There is not a single straight line or perfectly perpendicular wall or column in the whole building. All horizontal lines are slightly curved, and the columns are a little larger at the base than at the top. This subtle architecture gives the Parthenon, even today in ruins, a remarkable symmetry. The Parthenon was turned into a church during the Christian era and then was damaged badly in a war between the Greeks and Turks in 1687. The final desecration came in 1812 when Lord Elgin stripped off all the surviving sculptures and took them to England where they now are displayed beautifully in the British Museum in London.

When Paul and other ancients visited the acropolis, access to the summit was through a large monumental gateway called the propylaea. An earlier propylaea had been destroyed during the Persian Wars, and the year after the Parthenon was completed, Pericles began work on the new one. It has massive columns and a great marble roof, and today, visitors still go through this propylaea to the acropolis summit.

The Erechtheion is another awesome temple that still stands on the acropolis. It was built between 421 B.C. and 407 B.C. and was dedicated to Athena and Poseidon, the god of the sea. On the site where the temple now stands, according to Athenian legend, Athena and Poseidon struggled for possession of the city. Poseidon struck the rock with his trident, and sea water, symbolic of Athens' naval might, gushed forth. Athena then struck the rock with her spear, and an olive tree bearing fruit sprang up. The Athenians judged the olive tree more important, and Athena became their patron goddess. Later, to reconcile the two deities, the Athenians built the Erechtheion. It is best known for the six caryatids, beautifully sculptured maidens, who support the massive marble roof with their heads.

When Paul came to Athens, the monumental temples were a reminder of the city's past glory, and the city still was respected for its cultural and intellectual heritage. "It was made up of people who basked in the afterglow of Athens' intellectual glory. They lived on lectures. They were kept alive by a diet of speculation, argument, and discussion. They dealt in ideas as other people dealt in butter and eggs" *(Interpreter's Bible).*

The Areopagus (Mar's Hill) is a large outcropping of rock at the foot of the acropolis. It was dedicated to

Aeres, the god of war, and was the meeting place for Athens' oldest court. It was a meeting place, too, for those who "spent their time in nothing except telling or hearing something new" (Acts 17:21). When Paul came with his message about Jesus Christ, it was "something new" to the Epicurean and Stoic philosophers, and the stage was set for Paul's famous sermon about the unknown god.

Paul began his sermon by observing that the Athenians were "very religious" and that he had seen the objects of their worship. Paul probably had visited the Parthenon and Erechtheion. How impressive they must have been in Paul's day as the white pentelic marble glistening in the bright sun against the deep blue Mediterranean sky. But Paul also had seen an altar with the inscription, "To an unknown god," and with that inscription as a starting point, Paul told them about the one god about whom they knew nothing. Though the Greeks worshiped many gods, it may have been a common precaution to have an altar like the one at Athens, for in 1909 archaeologists found an altar inscribed "to unknown gods" at the temple of Demeter in Pergamum across the Aegean Sea from Athens.

There are three contrasts in Paul's sermon about the unknown god. First, there is the contrast between the one God who created the world and all things therein and the Epicurean philosophy of materialism and the eternity of matter. Second, Paul contrasts the God who does not dwell in temples made with hands with the Greek deities and their magnificent temples. Third, Paul describes a God who "made from one every nation of men to live on all the face of the earth," and this is in sharp contrast with the racial exclusiveness of the proud Greeks.

Some believed Paul's message, but others mocked. And Paul soon left Athens—without establishing an enduring church there, as far as we know—and went on to Corinth, where he found a sensual city more receptive than intellectual Athens had been.

REVIEW

1. How did the Mount of Olives play a central role in the New Testament? What were some of the events that occurred there?
2. What is the interesting resurrection tradition associated with the Mount of Olives?
3. What is the biblical significance of Coastal Caesarea?
4. What distinguished Coastal Caesarea even in its own time?
5. What significant find was discovered in Caesarea that referred to Pontius Pilate?
6. What was the Athens of Paul's day like?
7. What was Mar's Hill? Do you think it was fairly easy and safe for Paul to speak as he did there?

CHAPTER EIGHT

To the Ends of the Earth

The Temple of Apollo in Corinth. 8.1

Corinth
Bill Humble

Background Reading: *Acts 18:11–17; 1 Corinthians 1:1–17*

Paul preached at Corinth for 18 months during his second missionary journey, established the church there, and later wrote the letters to the church that we have in our New Testament known as 1 and 2 Corinthians. The second missionary journey began at Anti-

119

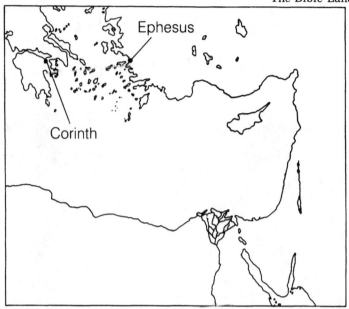

och in Syria as did each of Paul's three preaching trips.

Paul crossed Asia Minor where he visited the churches he had planted on the first preaching trip. Then he went to Iroas where he received his Macedonian call and crossed onto the continent of Europe for the first time. He preached at Philippi, Thessalonica and Beroea in Macedonia and then came to Athens alone where he confronted the Epicurean and Stoic philosophers with the great sermon about the one God who was unknown to the Greeks. After Athens, Paul traveled west 50 miles to Corinth, where he stayed for a year and a half.

Corinth was located at one of the most strategic crossroads of the ancient world. The city was situated on the narrow isthmus that was a natural gateway between southern Greece, called the Peloponnesus, and the north. The isthmus was also the gateway between the Saronic Gulf to the east and the Gulf of Corinth to the west.

The sea route around Cape Malea at the southern tip

of Greece was so treacherous and dangerous that an old proverb said, "When you go around Cape Malea, forget your home." Ship owners feared to risk their vessels on so dangerous a passage. Instead, they would unload their ships at the Isthmus of Corinth, transport the cargoes by land across the five-mile-wide isthmus, then reload them on vessels on the other side. When Corinth was at the zenith of its power in the sixth century B.C., a stone passageway called the *diolkos* was built across the isthmus, and smaller ships could be transported across the isthmus on rollers without being unloaded.

Ancient rulers dreamed of digging a canal across the Isthmus of Corinth, and under the Roman emperor Nero, work actually began. But it was too difficult an undertaking for ancient times, and the present Corinthian canal was not completed until 1893.

Corinth's strategic location meant that it commanded the overland trade routes between northern Greece and the Peloponnesus and the east-west sea routes that met at the Isthmus of Corinth. It was a busy cosmopolitan city in Paul's day with seamen and merchants from all parts of the Roman world meeting in Corinth.

Corinth reached the peak of its prosperity and power in the sixth century B.C. Philip of Macedon took control of Corinth in 338 B.C., and during the Hellenistic era, the city was a center of trade, commerce and pleasure for the seamen who passed through the city. Disaster came with the Romans. Corinth was destroyed by the Roman counsul Lucius Mummius in 146 B.C., the city razed and burned, and its citizens sold into slavery.

The site of Corinth lay in ruins for exactly a century until 46 B.C., when Julius Caesar recognized the strategic location of Corinth and decreed the rebuilding of the city. The new city soon had a cosmopolitan population that included local Greeks, freedmen who came as colonists from Italy, and many people, including Jews, who came from the East. The new Roman city grew rapidly under Augustus, became a commercial center again, and was made the Roman capital of Achaia. Thus, when Paul came to Corinth, he found himself in a busy new Roman city, where many trade routes of the ancient world met and where all the vices of a pagan seaport city flourished.

The American School of Classical Studies at Athens has carried on extensive excavations at Corinth since 1896, and the city they have uncovered is the Roman Corinth where Paul lived and preached for 18 months. Many of the streets and buildings that have been excavated are the ones that Paul knew.

The archaeologists have found a broad paved street, the Lechaeum Road, that entered the city from the sea, and Paul would have traveled on the Lechaeum Road many times. Corinth, like any Greek city, had a monumental gateway called the *propylea*. As a visitor entered Corinth through the *propylea,* he soon would have come to the famous fountain of Peirene. The fountain supplied water for the city and was surrounded in Paul's day with impressive public buildings.

Corinth had a large and busy agora or market place, the ancient world's equivalent of a shopping mall. The agora was surrounded with shops, and the archaeologists have restored one of these to give today's visitor an idea of what the agora looked like in the first century. According to the New Testament, Paul worked at his trade of tent making while he preached in Corinth (Acts 18:3), and this might have been at one of the shops around the agora.

A large platform, called the bema, was on one side of the agora. Covered with blue and white marble in Paul's day, the bema was where public meetings were held. If the Roman governor wanted to address the populace of the city, they would assemble around the bema to hear him. When the Jews assaulted Paul and dragged him before Governor Gallio, this took place at the bema (Acts 18:12). It is possible that Paul may have proclaimed the gospel from the bema earlier in his sojourn at Corinth.

There were two temples in first century Corinth that are of interest to students of the New Testament. One temple was to Aphrodite, the goddess of love. This temple was situated on the Acrocorinth, a mountain that towered 1,886 feet above the city. The Acrocorinth was strongly fortified and provided a refuge for the citizenry when enemy armies threatened, and these fortifications were so impregnable that they never were taken by storm.

And there was the temple of Aphrodite. It had a thousand priestesses, or "sacred slaves," who were prostitutes offering their services in the name of religion. When sailors arrived in Corinth after months at sea, the priestesses offered companionship and love in the name of Aphrodite. Thus, Corinth was noted for wealth and a sensual lifestyle. "To live like a Corinthian" became a synonym for immorality.

The other temple was located near the heart of the city and was dedicated to Apollo. This temple had been built about 540 B.C., a century before the Parthenon in Athens, and had been spared when the Romans destroyed Corinth in 146 B.C. It originally had 35 monolith columns, seven of which still are standing. These columns are unusual in that each one is cut from an enormous block of stone, while the columns at other Greek temples, like the Parthenon, are put together in sections called "drums."

With the temples of Aphrodite and Apollo dominating the life of Corinth, it is not surprising that Paul's letters to the church include many warnings against idolatry and the immorality that accompanied it. "Do you not know that your bodies are members of Christ? Shall I therefore take the members of Christ and make them members of a prostitute? Never!" (1 Corinthians 6:15).

Several archaeological discoveries at Corinth are of special interest in relation to Paul's ministry. One is the bema, or platform, where Paul was dragged before the governor Gallio. Earlier, it may have been the place where Paul preached to the Corinthians.

Another discovery is a large paving stone that has the inscription, "Erastus, in return for the aedileship, laid (the pavement) at his own expense." The book of Romans, written from Corinth on Paul's third missionary trip, includes a greeting from "Erastus, the city treasurer" (Romans 16:23). Scholars think it is probable that this city treasurer, evidently a Christian, was the same Erastus who laid the paving stone.

Yet another archeological discovery relates to Gallio, the Roman proconsul of Achaia while Paul was preaching in Corinth and the official before whom the Jews accused Paul of teaching people to "worship God contrary to the law." According to Acts 18, when Gallio judged that it was some kind of religious argument among Jews, he refused to consider the charges and drove them from the bema. An inscription found at Delphi in northern Greece in 1908 dates Gallio's rule in Corinth in 51 or 52. This fixed date has helped scholars work out a chronology for Paul's life.

Despite the immoral pagan culture in Corinth, Paul left a body of believers there. But not surprisingly, it was a congregation of Christians beset with serious problems. The church was divided into factions; there were lawsuits among brethren; and the church tolerated flagrant immorality. Other problems were related to idolatry, the Lord's Supper, spiritual gifts, and the resurrection of the dead.

Paul spent three years at Ephesus on his third missionary journey (Acts 19), and during that time he learned of the problems at Corinth and wrote the church a letter addressing the problems, which is our book of 1 Corinthians. Forced to leave Ephesus after the great riot (Acts 19), Paul went to Troas where he hoped to meet Titus and receive news from Corinth, but Titus was not there. He went on to Macedonia where he met Titus and received the happy news that the Corinthian brethren had repented and were working to solve their problems. Relieved and thankful, Paul wrote the church again (2 Corinthians) and followed his letter with a three-month visit to Achaia and Corinth (Acts 20:1–3).

The Library of Celsus in Ephesus.   8.2

Ephesus

Bill Humble

Background Reading: *Acts 18:18–21; Acts 19:1–20; 2 Timothy 1:16–18; Revelation 2:1–7*

Ephesus was the most important city in the Roman province of Asia (now western Turkey) in New Testament days. Located at the point where the Cayster River flowed into the Aegean Sea, Ephesus was important as a commercial and seaport city and a religious center with its great temple of Aretmis (Diana is the latin name for Artemis). The population was perhaps 250,000 or 300,000. Because the apostle Paul focused his preaching on the major cities of the empire, it is not surprising that he visited Ephesus briefly on his second missionary trip (Acts 18:19–21) and then returned on his third journey. We learn from his later address to the Ephesian elders that he had spent three years there (Acts 20:31), and this is Paul's longest residence in any city during his years of travel and evangelism.

The original settlement of Ephesus goes back at least to the 12th century B.C. when Ionian colonists from Greece settled on that site. Ephesus became a great commercial and seaport city, which was captured by the Persians and incorporated into their empire in 557 B.C. It was captured by Alexander the Great in the fourth century B.C. and then became a part of the Roman empire in 133 B.C.

Thus, when Paul came to Ephesus, it was one of the great cities of the Mediterranean world. The city's greatest days as a trade center were already past, though the magnificence of the city would hardly have betrayed that fact. The problem was that Ephesus' harbor was filling up with silt. The forests had been destroyed in the area drained by the Cayster River; there was extensive erosion; and silt was threatening the harbor. There were extensive efforts to clear the harbor during the reign of Emperor Domition just two or three decades after Paul's residence at Ephesus. But across the early Christian centuries, the battle to save the harbor was lost; the great city slowly declined. Whereas the broad Arcadian Way led down to the sea and wharves in Paul's day, now it is seven miles to the Aegean Sea. But even though the silting doomed the city's prosperity, the decline took centuries. The third great ecumenical council of the church was held at Ephesus in 431 A.D. The ruins of the double church of St. Mary where the council met still can be seen. In the sixth century, the Emperor Justinian built a great new church at Ephesus on the site where the apostle John was believed to be buried, and extensive ruins of this church still are standing.

Ephesus is an uninhabited ruin today, but the antiquities and monuments are among the most impressive anywhere in the Roman world. The Curetiae Street comes into the city from the northeast and leads to the heart of the city. The street is lined with the ruins of impressive public buildings and monuments. Among them is the odeon, a small theater seating about 1,500 that was used for concerts and for meetings of the Ephesus city council.

Ephesus had one of the three greatest libraries of the ancient world. The other two were at Alexandria and Pergamum. The Library of Celsus at Ephesus had been built by Julius Aquilla to honor his father, Celsus. Archaeologists have restored the facade of the Library of Celsus, and this is one of the most imposing monuments in the city. Scholars believe the hall of Tyrannus where Paul taught was somewhere near the library, so it is easy to visualize Paul using this great library during his years at Ephesus.

The three libraries at Ephesus, Pergamum and Alexandria were rivals. The Egyptians had a near-monopoly on the production of papyrus, the common ancient writing material, and when they forbade the export of papyrus, the libraries at Ephesus and Pergamum were threatened until parchment or thin leather became a durable alternative to papyrus.

The agora or marketplace of Ephesus was near the Library of Celsus and was the largest and most magnificant in the ancient world. Business of all kinds was transacted here, and among the merchants there were artisans who sold little silver shrines to the goddess Artemis.

The temple and worship of Artemis were the crowning glories of Ephesus. Religious pilgrims and tourists came from afar, and much of the city's prosperity was derived from supplying the needs of these pilgrims. Historical sources outside the Bible lend credence to the claim of the Ephesus town clerk that people everywhere knew "that the city of the Ephesians is temple keeper of the great Artemis, and of the sacred stone that fell from the sky" (Acts 19:35). Silver coins honoring Artemis were minted in many different countries, and these make it obvious that she was, indeed, worshiped all over the Roman world.

The cult of Artemis began at least 1,000 B.C. in a mother-goddess fertility cult in Asia Minor. Later, when Greek colonists settled in the area, they used the name of their goddess Artemis to describe the older fertility goddess, and the two religions were brought together in fertility rituals and religious prostitution. The many images of Artemis that have been uncovered always portray her as a many-breasted goddess. The first temple to Artemis was built at Ephesus by Croesus who reigned around 550 B.C. This temple was destroyed by fire in 356 B.C. on the very night, omen-watchers would later note, when Alexander the Great was born across the Aegean Sea in Macedon.

Alexander the Great's armies occupied Ephesus in 334 B.C., and it was Alexander who encouraged the building of a magnificent new temple to Artemis. This was the temple that was Ephesus' greatest glory in Paul's day and which we now remember as one of the seven wonders of the ancient world. The architecture of the temple of Artemis was similar to the Parthenon in Athens, but it was four times as large as the Parthenon and longer than a football field. It had a double row of columns, 127 in all, around it and was decorated with the sculptures of Pheidias, Praxiteles and Apelles.

The temple stood for more than 600 years and then was destroyed by the Goths in 260 A.D. The destruction was so complete that by modern times the site was forgotten, and it was not until 1870 that the ruins were discovered in a marshy area more than a mile from Ephesus. The British Museum has a number of column bases from the temple, each approximately seven feet in diameter and decorated with beautiful sculptures. Other columns may be seen in Istanbul, where they were carried from Ephesus and used in the building of St. Sophia church in the sixth century.

The temple and worship of Artemis were responsible for much of Ephesus' fame and fortune in New Testament times, but the good news about Jesus preached by Paul had such a powerful impact that it threatened those whose livelihood depended on Artemis-worship. According to the New Testament, Demetrius called a meeting of the silversmiths who made shrines of Artemis. He charged that Paul's preaching was turning people away from Artemis-worship, and he said, "There is danger not only that this trade of ours may come into disrepute but also that the temple of the great goddess Artemis may count for nothing, and that

129

she may even be deposed from her magnificence, she whom all Asia and the world worship" (Acts 19:27). The silversmiths were enraged and began shouting, "Great is Artemis of the Ephesians." The city was filled with confusion, and a great mob converged and rushed into the theater.

The great theater is still there, built into the low hills at the base of Mount Pion and with a seating capacity of about 25,000. As the modern visitor to the ruins of Ephesus climbs to the top of the theater and views the vast ruins of the ancient city spread out before him, he can easily visualize the theater filled with a shouting mob, many of whom didn't even know why they were there.

Ephesus had a considerable Jewish population in Paul's day, and they evidently feared that the mob's anger at Paul might threaten them. The Jews put forward one of their number, a man named Alexander, to make a defense. When the mob realized he was a Jew, they shouted for two hours, "Great is Diana of the Ephesians." Finally, the town clerk quieted the mob and told them the tumultous riot could not be justified and dismissed the assembly.

The New Testament record seems to indicate that Paul left Ephesus shortly after the riot. But he must have remembered the scene and wrote in 1 Corinthians 15:32, "I fought with beasts at Ephesus," perhaps a figurative reference to the ferocity of the devotees of Artemis.

Paul had an impact on Ephesus, both through his personal ministry there and the letter he later wrote from his Roman imprisonment, that never would be erased. Today, the once-great city is an uninhabited ruin, its monuments and antiquities a silent reminder of its former grandeur. The beautiful temple of Artemis, one of the seven wonders of the ancient world, is gone. Its site is marked only by one solitary column that has been restored. Artemis is worshiped no more, but the good news about Jesus Christ, proclaimed by Paul in ancient Ephesus, is still heard around the earth.

REVIEW

1. Why did Corinth hold such a prominent place in the New Testament world? What was it like in Paul's day?
2. Describe modern Corinth.
3. Why was the city of Corinth considered so immoral and corrupt? Is there a modern city that you would consider to be morally like Corinth?
4. What were some of the problems that beset the Christians at Corinth?
5. Why was Ephesus so important to the Romans? Why did it eventually decline?
6. Describe modern Ephesus.
7. Describe the impact the gospel had on Ephesus.

CPSIA information can be obtained
at www.ICGtesting.com
Printed in the USA
LVHW092337210619
622025LV00001B/11/P